SUCH A LONG JOURNEY

SUCH A LONG JOURNEY

A BIOGRAPHY OF GILBERT SHAW, PRIEST

by
R.D. Hacking

MOWBRAY
LONDON & OXFORD

First published 1988
by A.R. Mowbray & Co. Ltd,
Saint Thomas House, Becket Street,
Oxford OX1 1SJ

Typeset by DMD, 52 St Clements, Oxford
Printed and bound in Great Britain by
Redwood Burn Limited, Trowbridge, Wiltshire

British Library Cataloguing in Publication Data

Hacking, R.D. (Rodney Douglas)., 1953 –
Such a long journey.
1. Church of England. Shaw, Gilbert
I. Title
283'.092'4

ISBN 0–264–67158–9

Contents

Acknowledgements

I should like first of all to pay tribute to the enormous kindness, help and consideration which I have received in writing this book from Fr Gilbert's daughter, Lady Patricia Trend and her late husband, Lord Burke Trend. Their encouragement and friendship has meant a great deal. Lord Trend read the final manuscript before his death and offered a number of helpful and characteristically perceptive comments. Fr Gilbert's sons, Bill and John Shaw, were also most gracious in offering their time, help and support.

Mother Mary Clare SLG has inevitably been a key person and I should like to express thanks to her for the time she has been willing to give as well as for access to her private papers.

Little of the work would have been possible without the help provided by the present Mother-General of the community, Mother Jane SLG, who provided me with an almost complete set of Fr Gilbert's writings and gave access to many of the sisters whose remembrances, anecdotes and thoughts have helped me to grasp the significance of his years as warden to their community. In particular I should like to mention Sisters Edna Monica, Mary Kathleen, Jocelyn Mary and the late Sisters Ruth and Rachel Mary. SLG have also been gracious hosts on my visits to the convents at Fairacres and Boxmoor and more than anything else have given much prayerful attention to the work.

Canon Donald Allchin has provided both help and kindness at various stages for which I am most grateful, not least for his comments upon the manuscript. Metropolitan Anthony and Archimandrite Sophrony were both welcoming and offered great encouragement, as did Fr Percy Coleman, Dr Eric Mascall, the Revd Alec Vidler, the Revd David Shapland, the Rt Revd Gordon Roe, and the Rt Revd Peter Walker, my present Bishop, a memorable interview with whom on the subject of Fr Gilbert led directly to my present appointment. Mrs Vera Hodges was able to offer much help in dealing with Fr Gilbert's relationship with her late husband and the Moot, and her son Mr Paul Hodges kindly furnished me with photographs he had taken, as did Canon Lane, a student at Burgh from October 1927. I am grateful too for the support of Bishop Oliver Tomkins and Canon Alan Wilkinson and to the editor of the Church Times, Mr Bernard Palmer for his interest. Dr Elizabeth Briere of the Fellowship of St Alban and St Sergius was of great assistance in obtaining various articles. Mr Don Parrish was kind enough to come for a meeting in London and was willing to share his knowledge of Fr Gilbert's darker years.

Mr Eric St John Foti most kindly made available a word-processor and the staff of Original Norfolk Punch have been more than patient with my use of their time and photocopier.

Mr Christopher Liddle not only sought out important information on Fr Gilbert's family and legal activities, but has been a good friend and supporter throughout, offering shelter and hospitality on more than a few occasions and at every stage, encouragement.

Dr Robert Williams of Mowbrays provided some necessary hard thinking and positive comments upon an earlier version of the manuscript and I should like to thank him too for the great warmth with which he has supported the final time of writing as well as for daring to undertake the correction of my appalling grammar.

Fr Gregory CSWG has not only been my closest collaborator in the work on the book but also, as my own spiritual father, a continual source of support and sustenance, and I would also like to thank Brother Mark CSWG and the Revd John Musther for their own contributions to the enlargement of my understanding, and the whole community for their prayerful support.

The title of the biography comes from T.S. Eliot's 'Journey of the Magi'. Fr Gilbert and Eliot worked together for some years and I feel sure he would think it a compliment to find Eliot's words used in this way. I think, too, they capture the essential ambiguities of his life, for it was such a long journey.

For the past four years my family have had to learn to live with Fr Gilbert, and have even had to move house because of him. They have not merely borne it all with good humour but have offered continual support and encouragement, and so to Maggie, Cathy and Jenifer, the greatest thanks of all.

Upwell Rectory, Norfolk RH
All Saints Day 1987

Prologue

Waterloo Station in London is a somewhat unlikely setting for an important religious encounter and Mother Mary Clare SLG certainly expected nothing more from her appointment there than a way of filling in time before she caught the 3.15 train. This was in November 1957, and as Mother-General of the Anglican Sisters of the Love of God, she was on her way from the mother-house in Oxford to their convent in Burwash. A friend had suggested she might profitably use the time waiting for her connection to meet a priest who lived nearby. The priest was Gilbert Shaw, more than twenty years her senior, tall though somewhat frail, his white hair contrasting markedly with the black of the ever-present cassock.

If each had expected little more than an exchange of pleasantries they were to be surprised. Their conversation lasted almost four hours, Mother Mary Clare just managing to catch the 6.15 train but by then she knew that a rare spiritual bond had been formed. For both of them the meeting occasioned that profound sense of joy which follows the discovery of someone who can, as it were, 'speak our language'. Here in an unlikely setting, they spoke with mounting excitement of reparation, reconciliation and the contemplative life in the sure knowledge that they had encountered another who knew from experience the reality of which they spoke. For both the encounter was timely.

Mother Mary Clare had been head of her community for three years and was well aware that it had reached a watershed. Founded in 1906, it was one of a number of such communities of nuns within the Church of England to come into being in the late 19th and early 20th centuries, part of the Catholic revival which had begun following the so-called Oxford movement which had begun in 1833. The founder was Fr George Seymour Hollings SSJE (a member of the Society of St John the Evangelist, an Anglican religious community for men often referred to as the 'Cowley Fathers', their original community house being just off the Cowley Road in Oxford). He guided them through the earliest years as they made tentative steps towards becoming a contemplative community, the first such community for women in the Church of England, given above all to the life of prayer rather than engaging in active works in parishes or education. Following his death in 1915 (whilst celebrating Mass for the sisters in their little chapel, now the Chapter House) he was replaced by Fr Lucius Cary SSJE, who was widely acknowledged as a gifted spiritual director and well versed in the Carmelite tradition within which the new community appeared to stand. He enabled the sisters to formulate their rule and clarify their particular understanding of the monastic life.

The heart of the life of the new community lay in the commitment to prayer, both alone in the cell and corporately in the divine office, not least in the celebration of the night office, a practice maintained by the community to the present day. Under Fr Cary their numbers grew rapidly and in 1928 the community opened a daughter-house at Boxmoor (now part of Hemel Hempstead), followed by the convent at Burwash seven years later. There was also a lay association for friends and supporters to enable them to share in the work of prayer and receive support under the guidance of the community with their own disciplined spiritual life.

Mary Clare was elected Mother on 7 April 1954, by which time it was clear that as often happens when institutions reach a certain age the vision enshrined in the rule and constitution had ceased to animate as once it had. Fr Cary had died in 1950 and when in 1954 Mother Mary Frances who had worked closely with him for many years was forced to resign due to ill health, an era came to an end. Although the Cowley Fathers continued to act as wardens to the community, Mother Mary Clare knew that more than anything else, if the community were to flourish, it would require a new sense of direction and purpose. It is clear that she herself had much to offer in this respect but the real step forward was to come three years later on her journey to Burwash and the meeting on Waterloo Station.

The community of the Sisters of the Love of God has come to play an important part in the life of the Church of England. Numbers have grown and it has been able to adapt its life to meet contemporary needs. In part, at least, this is due to the injection of life and purpose resulting from the partnership of Gilbert Shaw and Mother Mary Clare in the ten years from 1957. Many people come to their houses for retreat, amongst them ordinands, priests, and bishops who take the opportunity to experience something of that depth of prayer such a community affords. By means of their own publishing house they also make available to an even wider audience aspects of the spiritual life of their own particular tradition.

Another significant development in the Church deriving from the partnership of Gilbert Shaw and Mother Mary Clare has been a rediscovery of the solitary life, women and men living alone as hermits or in communities of solitaries wholly given to a life of prayer. There has also appeared a major new community for men called to the contemplative life, the Community of the Servants of the Will of God (CSWG) at Crawley Down in Sussex, which has shown unusual growth and development at a time when some other religious communities for men have been in decline. This community claims Gilbert Shaw as one of its founders and its guiding theological light.

Nor has his influence been limited to the monastic domain. A number of writers within the charismatic movement regard him as one of their own predecessors in the exercise of unusual spiritual gifts and as amongst the most authoritative writers on matters related to the paranormal and the ministries of deliverance, including exorcism. Groups such as the Churches Fellowship for Psychic and Spiritual Studies also regard this work and teaching highly (though, somewhat ironically, he had attempted to have the group banned by the bishops at its inception).

Christian socialist groups hail the work he did in the East End of London during the 1930s as being amongst the most important initiatives in Church involvement with the unemployed, and something which fifty years later has particular significance in the context of renewed high unemployment. Just how important this work was can be seen from the fact that in 1984 a modern history exhibition organized by the Greater London Council in the Royal Festival Hall featured a stand highlighting some of Shaw's political activities in pre-war Poplar.

Outside the Anglican fold Orthodox Christians look to him as being amongst the few western writers and teachers whom they really felt they could communicate with and learn from. Often the least ecumenically-minded of Christians, they have at times spoken of him almost as one of their own. Indeed the Russian Archbishop Metropolitan Anthony has gone on record as saying that he regards Shaw as 'the greatest priest I have ever known in any tradition, Orthodox, Catholic or Anglican'.

However, it would have to be conceded that in 1957 Gilbert Shaw did not obviously manifest greatness nor, at least within his own Church, did he attract much in the way of attention. Now in his seventies and physically unwell it seemed more likely that his somewhat extraordinary career had come to a disappointing end. A man whose reputation as a spiritual director thirty years earlier had brought him up to two thousand penitents, whose work in the East End of London before the war had brought him renown and respect, was now largely ignored or dismissed as a dangerous eccentric. Even some of those with whom he worked let him down or abandoned him. There remained too the continuing pain of a marriage which had gone wrong almost from the beginning. For more than thirty years he and his wife had more or less lived apart, to such an extent that few people even knew he was married.

If he was now experiencing the loneliness of old age it was no more than the continuation of a life-time pattern. At times there seemed a certain perversity about his independence but it was probably this which had enabled him to swim against the many prevailing tides which characterized the Church of England in his lifetime. The great concerns of his life, prayer and the life of the spirit, did not feature prominently in the public proceedings of a Church which seemed more interested in the exigences of ecclesiastical machination, whether of the perennial Church–State kind or the introspective reformation of law and liturgy. Of course there were others concerned with prayer and the like but not quite in the same way, with the particular theological emphases which drew the Orthodox to him and were to manifest themselves through SLG. And if these things set him apart, even more isolating was his involvement in the somewhat seamier world of the paranormal, something understood then even less than now. In all these ways, as in his espousal of the pacifist cause in the second world war or the way he set about his work in the East End, he either chose to be or found himself standing alone.

It is no small testimony to the spiritual perspicacity of Mary Clare that she recognized the qualities of this somewhat frail old man. What is certain is that something 'clicked' between them. John V. Taylor has given the name 'Go-Between God' to the mysterious power which enables communication between strangers and which can turn an encounter into a meeting. Whatever occasioned this particular conjunction made possible the establishment of an intimate relationship which for Shaw at least, brought a genuine sense of fulfilment and the resolution of many of the tensions with which he had lived since childhood. It was also the beginning of a partnership which would enable that flowering of his life-work which gives cause for him to be remembered and makes him worthy of attention.

As he would no doubt see it, the primary significance of his life and work lies in that which God worked through him and continues to be of importance in the Church. But the circumstances of his life also provide an interesting and clear example of grace at work in and through the vagaries of a complex and, at times, eccentric nature. By the end it did seem to have a meaning hardly guessable at in 1957. Finally, it also serves as a kind of counterpoint to the main themes of Church life in the first half of the century, an insight into some of the unusual motifs which undergird the principal melody and give it substance.

1

The Long Beginning
1886–1924

Early Years

Gilbert Shuldham Shaw was born on 10 July 1886 in Dublin into a family with both wealth and good connections. His father, Joseph Shaw Q.C. served as a Parliamentary Advocate and, in addition to a directorship with the Great Western Railway, had inherited a holding in a Welsh mining company from which he drew a considerable income.

The good connections came from his mother Charlotte Blanche, née Smyly. Eminent lawyers and medical men were numbered among her forebears whilst her father Sir Philip Crampton Smyly was honorary physician to both Queen Victoria and King Edward VII, President of the Royal College of Surgeons in Ireland and a member of the General Medical Council. He had married Nina, daughter of the third Baron Plunket, and sister to the Archbishop of Dublin, who baptized Gilbert. Charlotte was the eldest of eight children and the portrait of her in Wolfson College, Cambridge, is a testimony to her striking beauty.

Whatever other benefits wealth and family may have brought, a happy childhood was not among them. Brought to London soon after baptism, Gilbert's earliest years were characterized by ill health. He was regarded as a delicate child and in need of constant attention, though most of this had to come from a succession of nurses, his mother being herself too ill to give him adequate care. Charlotte's physical state worsened perceptibly after the birth of a daughter, Muriel, in 1891 and with the intention of ministering to both mother and son, Joseph rented property in Wensleydale, in the North Riding of Yorkshire. Gilbert was to spend considerable periods of time there, attending school at Jervaulx, alongside the ruins of the Cistercian Abbey. Increasingly however his mother was too ill to leave London and it was left to various aunts and governesses to attend to Gilbert and his sister.

In 1895 he began to attend school in London, and two years later he was taken to his first prep. school, Arnold's, at Wixenfield. Before leaving with his father to make the journey, he made what was to be his last visit to his mother, for within a few weeks she died. On the day of the funeral he was put on a train, met at the station and taken home where he discovered an open coffin in the dining room and his father pacing up and down in silence. After the funeral he was taken back to the railway station and returned to school. The most he could recall was his father saying that his mother had gone on a long journey and that one day he would follow. It is hardly surprising that almost at once he became ill, suffering in the following months from whooping cough and rheumatic fever and spending most of his time in the nearby sanatorium.

In 1900 he was successful in the entrance examinations for Eton where he began in the Easter half, though this brought no relief to the gloom of his life and the only enjoyment he seems to have known was in the holidays when he found solace in the beauty of the countryside. His father continued to rent large country houses for their use and Gilbert would go for long walks with the gamekeeper and learn how to use a gun. He also developed a love for books and began to read widely in the fields of history and literature, a passion for which he retained throughout his life.

With the return to school in the autumn unhappiness returned. In part his physical weaknesses, coupled to a slight speech impediment made him something of a butt for the jokes of others and he experienced some bullying. On one occasion he recalled being fixed into a folding bed and his feet beaten by six of his peers though on being released he did at least strike back, thrashing those about him with a brass candlestick, discovering and revealing a violence and strength which shook his taunters and himself. They fled and never returned, and the event marked a slight watershed for Gilbert. He was able to change house and for the first time received something resembling care from a new housemaster.

It is no doubt unwise to be over-assertive in claims made about the long-term psychological effects of childhood experience but we know enough not to discount them. Certainly Gilbert's earliest experiences of loneliness and bereavement must have left their marks upon him, and perhaps account for his heightened awareness of the darker side of life, and in some measure for his predilection for the writings of St John of the Cross.

The summer of 1901 provided Gilbert with the first real opportunity to get to know his father. Joseph had rented Forcett Hall, an imposing residence in the North Riding of Yorkshire, and for some weeks was able to introduce Gilbert to fishing, horse driving and above all photography, in which he was to remain actively interested throughout his life. In later years he took a professional course in the art and science of photography, manifesting a considerable talent with the camera and experimenting with colour and special effects long before these were commonplace. It was fortunate that Gilbert had such things to occupy his time for Forcett Hall was an isolated and bleak place. The village of Forcett is remote and unwelcoming to this day. Situated to the north of the Yorkshire Dales it has neither their beauty nor does it enjoy their protection from the bitterly cold northern winds that sweep down in winter. The hall itself is an ugly and formidable building with outhouses and an ornamental lake, and perhaps just made bearable by possessing a better than average library into which Gilbert was glad to make the occasional foray.

Gilbert was confirmed at school in 1902 after only one preparation session. Although he had won a prize at prep. school for scripture knowledge he later acknowledged that school religion left him with more of a distaste for religion than a desire to know more. Forcett Parish Church similarly held little to command his attention although he admitted an interest in the Psalms and the Athanasian Creed. But if religion brought him little consolation, improving health meant he was at last able to participate in games at school in which he enjoyed some moderate success. As he grew older he began to appreciate school and the opportunities it provided. His speech defect began to wane and in addition to winning prizes for photography he passed Cambridge Entrance examinations a year early. He received awards for History essays and then belied his previous reputation by winning house athletic competitions.

Among the opportunities provided by Eton was the possibility of spending time in the East End of London in the school Mission House. Gilbert paid his first visit to Hackney in 1903 and was greatly shocked by what he saw. It led him to give up his Christmas holiday of 1903–4 and he and a friend used this time to run a youth club for children of the unemployed, of whom there were many. In 1905 after leaving school he spent the summer in Hackney, employed by a group known as the Charity Organization as an investigator, testing for T.B. those wishing to emigrate to Canada. To his horror he found that there was tuberculosis in almost every house, that children were dying for want of the most basic medical care and that in the absence of dole there were men and women whose only clothing was made from old sacks sewn together.

These experiences were to stand Gilbert in good stead almost 30 years later when he came to live in the East End. In these early days, to those who had come from the privileged ranks of Eton College, charity seemed the only possible response and only later did Gilbert's experience lead him to see the need for corporate action. In 1905 it was no doubt good form for younger members of the privileged class to concern themselves with bettering the lot of the poor, to which the existence of school missions bears witness, but Gilbert was already exhibiting a greater sense of commitment than many of his peers. In later life he was to be highly critical of those from the upper classes who from the security of their drawing rooms paid the occasional visit to dispense charity to the poor.

Cambridge

In the autumn of 1906 Gilbert went up to Cambridge to read History at Trinity. He won the freshmen's prize and after an initial period of anxiety and troubled sleep, began to enjoy the intellectual demands of college life. He took elocution lessons and, with some success, spoke in debates as well as developing his interest in literature.

University religion proved no more appealing than that of school, though perhaps being true to his social upbringing he would attend chapel on festival days and it was on one such occasion that Gilbert's life was to be transformed. On Ascension Day, 24 May 1906, he attended the celebration of Holy Communion in the college chapel and experienced something which brought to him an awareness of a whole new dimension in which he could know the reality of God. He was profoundly affected by this experience and began to attend chapel regularly whilst investigating the Christian societies in the University although he was not over-impressed with what he discovered and it was only when a new

Precentor came to Trinity almost 18 months later in the autumn of 1907 that his new faith began to grow.

John How had returned to Cambridge having served his title in south London, and after a year's lectureship in Hebrew at St John's he received the offer of the Precentorship at Trinity. In later years he was a founding father and Superior of the Oratory of the Good Shepherd, an anglican catholic association for celibate men and he ran their Cambridge house until he married. After periods as diocesan missioner in Manchester under William Temple and then as vicar of Liverpool, he became Bishop of Glasgow and Galloway and Primus of the Scottish Episcopal Church. Cambridge has traditionally been more associated with the evangelical wing of the Church of England, catholics favouring Oxford, but How was one of the leaders of that liberal-catholic group which endeavoured to maintain a presence within the University. Many priests were to come to owe a great deal to John How's influence in Cambridge, and Gilbert Shaw was among the earliest group although it seems likely from the fact that no mention is made of him in How's diaries that Gilbert did not push himself to the fore.

Together they visited the Trinity College Mission in Camberwell and drew up plans for a mission there during the Christmas vacation. Gilbert's understanding and grasp of the faith was growing rapidly throughout this period and he arranged for W.B. Trevelyan to come from Liddon House to conduct a quiet day in Trinity chapel for the missioners. Almost forty undergraduates took part in the mission. Mornings were given over to factory visiting and home calls were made in the afternoons. Each evening there was a procession throughout the streets followed by a mission service for men. These Missions placed a strong emphasis on the Sacraments and at the end of the mission Gilbert made his first confession.

He now spent less and less time at home. His father no longer maintained the house in Yorkshire and instead rented property at Brampton Bryan, near Ludlow. Gilbert paid a brief visit over Christmas, enjoying some shooting and fishing, but wanted to spend some more time in Camberwell before term began. During 1907 he became a member of the newly-founded Church Society together with Will Spens, then of Selwyn and later Master of Corpus Christi. The two became great friends and each Sunday invited a major scholar to lunch, after which they would take their guest for a vigorous constitutional, during which they would quiz him on aspects of the faith in relation to his particular discipline.

In some ways he stood apart from his fellow Anglo-Catholics. He was much less 'churchy' than many of them and his experiences in Camberwell, on top of the earlier visits to Hackney, now led him to be much more interested in political matters. He became a member of the Independent Conservative Club in the University and began to engage in political activities within the city of Cambridge. Thus, from the very beginning of his life as a Christian, Gilbert revealed an active social and political involvement to be a major strand in his understanding of faith.

In 1908 his thinking about such matters received its greatest boost from the Hulsean lectures of J. Neville Figgis, a member of the anglican monastic Community of the Resurrection in Mirfield, formerly a history don in the University and arguably among the most important, if largely neglected, anglican theologians of the century. The lectures were given under the title 'The Gospel and Human Needs', and spoke directly to Gilbert's experiences in London. In later life Gilbert saw the lectures as a prophetic insight into the failure of the church to speak effectively to what he called 'the over-ripe civilization of the pre-First World War days before its autumn luxuriousness of Romantic idealism and Baroque emotionalism was brought to judgement'. Figgis helped Gilbert set his faith and political awareness within a theoretical framework which never allowed their division. Even in his teaching about the nature of spiritual warfare at the end of his life, it is constantly within the actual historical contexts of living that Gilbert expected such conflict to be understood and when Figgis began his addresses with the words 'Christ calls not to peaceful days and quiet nights, but to the heights and depths of sacrifice' Gilbert knew that they should not be understood merely metaphorically. An authentic ministry anywhere, especially amongst the poor, would always be costly.

Gilbert's concern for politics led him to opt for an extra year in Cambridge to read Economics in addition to Part II of the History Tripos. It was at this time that he began to come under pressure from his father to follow him into the law and he began to make regular visits to London and dinner at the Inner Temple, although it is clear that the possibility of ordination was also in his mind.

Cambridge provided the setting for an encounter which ultimately was to play an enormous part in Gilbert's later life and ministry. The last decade of the 19th century had seen a revival of interest in ancient religion, witchcraft and the occult. Under the influence of men such as C.W. Leadbeater, quasi-religions such as Theosophy flourished, seeking to combine Indian religious writings with magic and philosophy. In many circles there was a significant romantic interest generated by such matters, not least in the universities. Among those who had built up a following for themselves as a 'high priest' of such matters was Aleister Crowley. He claimed to be a master magician and had begun his own magical order, the AA. In 1908, his eminence at its height, Crowley came to visit some of his followers in Cambridge, and amongst those who came to hear him was Gilbert Shaw.

For some time previous he had begun to be aware within himself of what he imagined to be an unusual psychic perception and it was after various odd experiences which he could not explain that he decided to make the effort to go and listen to Crowley. It is clear that Crowley fascinated many of his listeners with his talk of paganism and magic. For many it was no doubt the romantic combination of mystery and the forbidden which held them, but others were drawn much more powerfully to Crowley himself. He offered an intellectual system allied to a means to power, a combination which some found irresistible, though his ability to draw people was not merely intellectual. He was also undoubtedly possessed of a strong psychic energy which when allied to a powerful personality gave him another level of influence over those who, though psychically sensitive, did not possess the same strength of will. Sex, alcohol and drugs were also inducements to neophytes, of whom he was to have many. He came to identify himself as '666' – the 'great beast' of the Book of Revelation and his subsequent career singles him out as an extremely unpleasant man who abused any number of his fellow humans especially a collection of women who in their fascination for him gave themselves body and soul, some of them bearing his children.

It is difficult to assess the effect upon Gilbert of his initial encounter with Crowley. In later life he was quite sure about the evil of the man, although he was to discover that his claims to power within the world of magic were exaggerations compared with some whom he was to encounter. Clearly Gilbert was stimulated by him at both the intellectual and psychic level. Perhaps it was his new-found faith which constrained him against further involvement, or that his own sharp psychic perception alerted him to what Crowley was doing. Whichever it was, Gilbert never took up with Crowley, but nevertheless did begin his own study of the occult beginning with a course in Primitive Greek Religion which he obtained special permission to attend.

Involvement with psychic practice and theory was to be a major feature of Gilbert's life and will be the concern of later pages. At this stage it was one of three major influences upon the young man, which together with faith and politics were to remain dominant in his life at least until after 1945. At various times one or other of these strands seemed to predominate and he was undoubtedly very confused about his future. Only later, when he was able to find a synthesis of faith and intellectual ideology in the writings of St John of the Cross did he begin to work towards a resolution of his inner conflicts, though it would be a process lasting many years.

Political activity took up much of his remaining time at Trinity and as President of the New Carlton Club he met with many senior political figures. He appears to have made a significant impression on F.E. Smith, later Lord Birkenhead, for after a dinner organized in his honour by Gilbert, a Government whip visited him suggesting the possibility that he become a Parliamentary candidate. Only 23 years old, it is a sign of the impact that he had already made, and he was tempted by the offer; but the question of ordination and pressure from his father with regard to the law meant that he felt he needed time to consider the possibilities. In consequence, after successfully completing Part II Economics, he decided to take advantage of an invitation to visit a cousin in New Zealand and to observe at first-hand what was then being hailed as the most advanced Labour government in the world.

Gilbert set sail in September 1909, intending to stay until the following February, but on the outward journey fell in with a Major-General Barron, Governor-designate of Tasmania and accepted his invitation to join his staff as junior ADC and early in 1910, his cadet uniform having been sent on from England, Gilbert began this new work. He enjoyed his time in Tasmania, vivid memories of which he could recall in old age though not least of its attractions was the space that it gave him for unhurried thought about his future.

Called to the Bar

Gilbert arrived home on Christmas Eve 1910. Although he was still torn about whether to go to the Bar or be ordained, at least by now he knew that he did not want a political career. Almost at once he began to take steps towards the Bar, eating dinners in the Inner Temple and gaining experience of the law in action in the solicitors' office of the London and North West Railway. In spare time between law examinations he returned to the mission in Camberwell and had experience of preaching, both at mission services and in the open air. Pressure from his family, and the need for financial support necessitated a choice and as ordination did not seem a practical possibility at this stage he continued in the direction of the Bar to which he was called in 1913, entering the Eustace Hill Chambers. Almost at once, perhaps through family contacts, he received a fair amount of work and within a short time had earned himself a good reputation. At this stage it did appear that the law now held him, and this was further confirmed when he married into a good legal family.

His bride was Sylvia Mary Smyly, whose acquaintance he had made on the day of his return from Tasmania, she being a houseguest of his sister Muriel. Bearing the same surname as his mother, she was a distant cousin and although five years younger than he, was actually a generation older: her great-grandfather was Gilbert's great-great-grandfather. Such an occurrence was not uncommon at a time when families were much larger than is the custom nowadays.

Sylvia's grandfather had followed his father into the law, as did her father William Cecil Smyly who became a County Court Judge. Thus as the daughter of a judge and with two brothers at the Bar, Sylvia was marrying into a home and lifestyle with which she was familiar. The report in *The Times* spoke of Gilbert as a 'promising barrister' and it was a great society event. Held in St Saviour's, St George's Square on 22 July 1913, it was conducted by the Bishop of London, Arthur Winnington-Ingram. Outwardly it appeared the ideal match which should have marked the beginning of a notable career in public life. That it did not, lay in the unresolved tensions within Gilbert, which like those rumbling in the heart of Europe, were only to become open in the following year.

Up to the outbreak of the war he continued to be busy and successful in his work. Their first child, John, was born in May and whilst the young family were on holiday in Herefordshire war was declared. Gilbert was caught up in the patriotic passion which characterized the early days of the war and even helped to organize a recruitment campaign in Hereford before returning to London. After tidying up his legal work, through the good offices of a friend, he secured a commission in the No.2 Company of the 5th City of London Artillery Regiment.

The army presented itself to Gilbert as an honourable means of escape from the law and he was never to practise again. Just one year had been enough to realize that this was not right for him. As it was, circumstances would have allowed his return to the Bar within a short space of time for Gilbert was never to see action. In the Spring of 1915, shortly before his regiment was due to go to France, he was thrown from his horse whilst out at exercise. As he fell, the horse kicked his head and he was seriously concussed, leaving him with recurring dizziness and mental disorder. The army was left with no alternative but to invalid him out. The circumstances were almost identical to those fifteen years earlier when the young Dick Sheppard, on his way to take up a commission in

South Africa, had been similarly thrown from a horse and invalided out of the army.

Gilbert made only slow progress towards recovery. He responded well to the psychiatric help offered him through-out 1915 but it was not until 1916 that he felt well enough to begin work once again. He and Sylvia had moved to Newbury where he entered government service as an enforcement officer in the South Midland Division with special responsibility for food distribution. He also became a member of the Borough Council and an active member of St John's Church in the town. It seems likely that Gilbert made use of his accident and subsequent illness as an excuse for not returning to the law, something which Sylvia and the family could hardly question. It would be different after the war when he would be put under considerable pressure to return but in wartime all sorts of things had to be accepted.

John of the Cross and William of Glasshampton

In Newbury he became good friends with the curate of St John's, the Revd Harris (Hugh) Trotter, formerly a roman catholic lay monk, who had been ordained as an Anglican to serve in Canning Town in 1911. This friendship led to one of the major influences upon Gilbert's life, for it was he who introduced Gilbert to the writings of St John of the Cross and opened up for him the entire Carmelite tradition. Although he had continued his own study of the faith, it was not until this moment that he found something to which he could commit himself intellectually, emotionally and at the spiritual/psychic level too, and it marks the point of departure for what was to become the main journey of his life.

Hugh Trotter acted as Gilbert's confessor and director for the next eight years. He was a good friend to the whole family and became godfather to their second son Bill who was born in June 1917. Later he served in various London churches before moving to Yorkshire as chaplain to the sisters of the Order of the Holy Paraclete in Whitby.

Gilbert was elected to represent Newbury Deanery at the Oxford diocesan conference on the National Mission of Repentance and Hope. The Mission was the Church's attempt to respond to the criticisms of those who suggested that she had failed to offer anything positive to the nation in the face of crisis. Archbishop Lang of York had expressed the hopes behind the Mission in an address to Convocation in 1916:

> We have called it a National Mission of Repentance and Hope; Repentance because we are called to bid men and women everywhere to repent of the sins which have stained our civilization and brought upon it the manifest judgement of God; and Hope because, during the closing period of this terrific ordeal in the midst of increasing strain and sacrifice and sorrow, our people will need the strength of Hope, and in those difficult days that are coming, when the old order will have gone and the duty will be laid upon the nation of seeking a new order in a new world, we must present before the minds of the nation the one hope, Christ, His Mind, His Spirit, for the rebuilding of a new world.

Such sentiments could not prevent the National Mission being a manifest failure though it cannot have been easy for anyone to voice criticism of it at the time of its inception. Perhaps by virtue of his being a layman Gilbert was better placed to be honest about his feelings than might have been some clergy and he gave voice to his criticisms at the diocesan conference. First, he felt the spiritual conception of the Mission to be inadequately founded. Appeals to moral virtue even with some religious language thrown in did not thereby cease to be Pelagianism. Second, as one of the few ex-soldiers present, he believed it unlikely to prove effective in communicating with the men whom he had come to know during his short period of service. Variations of these two criticisms were ultimately to emerge from a variety of sources and already in 1916 they found resonance within Charles Gore, the Bishop of Oxford. He supported Gilbert as did other speakers including the new Superior of the Cowley Fathers, Fr Bull SSJE.

As a result of his contributions to the debates Bishop Gore co-opted Gilbert onto the diocesan executive of the Mission and pressed him into considering ordination. Although this appealed to Gilbert, he did not yet feel sufficiently able to proceed in the face of the opposition if engendered within the family. Not that Sylvia was intrinsically opposed to the church; throughout her life she remained a most devout woman and was very active within the Mothers Union at local and national levels, but she did want to see Gilbert back at the Bar. She had hoped that the termination of the war would provide the opportunity for this and indeed early in 1919 Gilbert was offered considerable financial incentives by his father to resume his legal career. He was not to be persuaded. Instead, following the birth of their daughter Patricia in the summer of that year, Gilbert took the family to Yattenden, near Reading and began work as a farmer with a friend with whom he entered into partnership.

In many ways it was a bizarre move and indicative of his very confused state of mind, a prevarication which sounds odd to those, who only knowing him in later life, recall a single-minded man with an almost iron will. If there is a single reason it can probably be found in the relationship with his father. Joseph was clearly determined that Gilbert should practise at the Bar and had continued to place considerable pressure upon him in this respect for many years, not least in keeping him financially dependent. With a young family to maintain Gilbert was not in a position wholly to cut himself from this in order to begin preparation for ordination. On the other hand, neither was he willing to countenance a return to the Bar. As it was he knew next to nothing about farming and although he was willing to be innovative (he was amongst the first in the area to use things such as mechanical tractors), almost at once he ran into financial problems and had to borrow considerable sums from his father to remain viable. Somewhat inevitably, the relationship between father and son, which had never been close was placed under even greater strain and following his eventual ordination broke down completely.

Gilbert's heart and soul were never in his farming and increasingly he was pre-occupied with church work. In 1919 the diocesan missioner Fr Karney appointed him as secretary of the diocesan Council for Evangelism. For the next three years Gilbert was kept active in this work which involved planning missions and the preparation of missioners to serve them.

From this time he began to make regular visits to the monastery of St Mary at the Cross, Glasshampton, the home of Fr William Sirr. Fr William had once lived in the East End of London as a priest in a community known as the Society of the Divine Compassion, an early anglican attempt at setting up a Franciscan community for men, which engaged in teaching, preaching and other active works, especially in areas of poverty and unemployment. Photographs exist showing Fr William leading unemployment marches in 1906. He spent fourteen years as a member of SDC, including six as Superior, but gradually there grew within him a sense that he was being called to a greater degree of prayer than seemed possible in an active community. As no such contemplative community for men existed he pressed for release from SDC to be allowed to found one. The process of departure was slow and tortuous and included a period spent living with the Cowley Fathers, but finally in 1918 with the support of a new Superior in SDC, Fr William was given permission to begin a new foundation in an isolated and ruined stable at Glasshampton in Worcestershire.

Fr William lived in Glasshampton until 1936 and although he remained convinced that God was bringing into being a contemplative community of which he was the forerunner, he was never to see that community come into being. From time to time men came and tested their vocation, but the life was extremely austere and none stayed. It seems likely that Gilbert came to know Fr William through Fr Bull SSJE, who as Superior of the Cowley Fathers had known Fr William during his years with them. William was to play a significant part in developing Gilbert's understanding of the contemplative life, a debt he frequently acknowledged.

Gilbert was responsible for selecting and training missioners to help with various diocesan missions and not infrequently he turned to undergraduates in Oxford. Among them was Derwas Chitty, who in later years was to be a notable scholar of the history and development of primitive monasticism; another was Max Petitpierre who was to work closely with Gilbert for many years in matters connected with the ministries of deliverance. In later years Max became a Benedictine monk at Nashdom Abbey, Bucks., taking the name of Dom Robert.

The first mission organized by Gilbert was at Bicester in 1921, followed by another at Eynsham and then, outside the diocese, at Glastonbury. The missions took a very traditional form, based on worship and preaching, a style later to be used to good effect by the Mirfield Fathers, though sometimes mistakenly thought only to be the province of evangelicals. Gilbert already had experience of leading such missions in Camberwell and so was well equipped to deal with the gentler areas of Oxfordshire.

Mounting tension

The success which Gilbert enjoyed in his work as missioner exacerbated the conflicts and tensions of both his inner and outer life. He was spending more and more time away from home, neglecting the farm and in the process losing the money his father had given to support them. Tensions between himself and Sylvia were also heightened by his frequent absences as well as the continuing disagreement between them on the matter of ordination and his return to the Bar. Within himself the call to ordination was growing ever stronger, the more so as he soaked himself in the works of St John of the Cross and paid visits to Glasshampton. He was also disturbed at the widening gap between himself and his father and there were a number of bitter arguments between them. It is not altogether surprising then, that in August 1922 these tensions finally came to a head and erupted.

The occasion of what was to be a serious nervous breakdown arose in the context of some follow-up work to the mission in Eynsham. Gilbert was working with Max Petitpierre and in the course of their days together each disclosed to the other something of the sharp psychic awareness they now discovered they had in common. It had been for them both a significant moment for then as now it is not always easy to know to whom to speak of such things. Most clergy would have been at a loss to know what to make of their awareness and experiences and at that time there was no Church group in existence to help them. In the absence of such guidance their own inexperience was now to lead them into trouble. Both had been aware of some kind of psychic disturbance associated with an ancient Roman settlement on the outskirts of the town and they set out to investigate. In later life neither was willing to speak about what they had encountered other than to say that they uncovered something evil which gave them a terrible fright – 'I once had my nose bitten by the devil' was how Gilbert described it. In the course of his later work his experience at Eynsham would prove valuable in making him fully aware of the nature of what he was up against in the reality of evil but at the time it triggered off a mental collapse.

He was bed-bound for some weeks without sign of improvement and only when he took up an invitation to visit South Africa, where his former friend Fr Karney was now Bishop of Johannesburg, did he being to show signs of recovery. He set sail in November and remained there five months. He enjoyed the visit and the opportunity it provided for him to see mission work undertaken in a variety of different contexts. For a while he lived in one of the theological colleges of the Community of the Resurrection, the community founded by Gore and of which Figgis had been a member. He enjoyed living under the Rule of the community and learned a great deal about the value and significance of silence and an ordered timetable. In later years he claimed that it was this order and silence which enabled an honest encounter with the tensions within himself. It provided an opportunity to stand completely back, remote from the pressures of home and family, consider his future and make the decision that on his return to England he would at once seek ordination.

He returned after Easter in 1923 and with the support of Bishop Gore, applied for and was offered a place for the following year at Westcott House, a theological college in Cambridge. By now Sylvia was resigned to his being ordained and she must have realized that further opposition was pointless. The experience of the previous months had strengthened Gilbert's will but it also brought about a major change in the relationship with his wife. Living in community, even for a short while, brought him to a position in which he did not know how he could reconcile being married with his call to the priesthood and its consequent commitment to the life of prayer. The situation was not helped by the growing breach between himself and Sylvia brought about by the conflicts of the previous years. As a result Gilbert decided to make a commitment to voluntary celibacy from the time of his return from South Africa. Although this was not wholly unknown in certain Anglo-Catholic circles and may in any case have been no more than the spiritual ratification of an existing breakdown in their marital relationship, it suggests a certain confusion about the place of sex in the life of Christians – though he was by no means alone in that. Having spent time with celibates in South Africa and relating at a spiritual level to unmarried priests or monks can hardly be said to have predisposed him to seeing a positive role to the place of sex in the spiritual life. It is clear that Gilbert Shaw never really came to terms with marriage throughout his entire ministry, whether his own or that of others, especially priests', and from 1924, with the exception of two years at the beginning of the war, he and Sylvia lived apart, Gilbert paying a weekly visit if convenient.

Sylvia was of course deeply hurt by all of this. She had already been forced to look after three small children in circumstances very much reduced from those with which she was familiar and from now on she was going to have to manage permanently without the husband and father of the family. Not unnaturally the rest of the family took her side, and Joseph Shaw in particular was angry with his son. Not only was he now abandoning his wife, but he had wasted his opportunities at the Bar and been guilty of unpropitious handling of money in the farming episode. It was something from which their relationship never recovered. In 1926 his father re-married, his new wife being none other than the sister of Gilbert's mother, his aunt Constance. It is a sign of what had happened between father and son that Gilbert was only informed after the wedding had taken place, and that after Joseph's death in 1933 the terms of his will prevented Gilbert from ever having access to his father's money other than in an initial small bequest. There was to be no reconciliation between them before Joseph's death.

Somehow or other in spite of the circumstances of their parents' relationship the three Shaw children seem to have grown up quite normally and although they did not see a great deal of their father they remained close to him. This is no small tribute to their mother and some of those who knew both her and Gilbert have commented that if ever there was a saint in the family it was Sylvia.

Gilbert used the period before going to Westcott House as a time of extended retreat. He prepared some notes on prayer which were published in 1924 under the title *A Pilgrim's Meed of Prayer and Praise* and for the first time enjoyed a period of inner peace. He was now thirty-seven, and although it had taken a mighty effort and had come by a somewhat circuitous route, it did seem as if his life and work were now about to fall properly into place and that his experience of tension and inner conflict had come to an end.

It was not to be so. Early in January 1924 he received a letter inviting him to become Vice-Principal of St Paul's Missionary College, Burgh in Lincolnshire. He had been recommended to the Principal, Canon Walter Boulter, by Bishop Karney and he was being asked to be senior full-time member of staff with responsibility for college discipline and the spiritual development of the students. The letter also made clear that the Bishop of Lincoln had agreed to his being ordained as a member of the College staff.

The invitation was quite unexpected although he had already acquired something of a reputation beyond the Oxford diocese as a missioner and speaker on spiritual matters. Although he had lived with considerable tensions within himself he had largely managed to keep them private and, outwardly at least, to his striking good looks was added an apparently supreme self-confidence which many would later think of as arrogance. His legal training stood him in good stead as a public speaker and to the end of his days he almost always adopted the manner of a barrister when addressing an audience or congregation. There would be many who did not like this, but to others it was compelling.

He decided to accept the invitation and in the autumn of 1924 set off for the Lincolnshire Wolds. The preparation was now complete. It had been a long beginning but the time had come for the next stage of his life. Those influences which were to dominate his ministry were by now at work within him. He had eight years of familiarity with the writings of St John of the Cross behind him, experience of the monastic tradition in two different forms and a considerable understanding of mission in its various forms. He knew too about the darker side of the spiritual life. Above all he brought to his ordination a powerful sense of the reality of God, something which he had come to know not just in 'spiritual' experiences of various kinds, but which had been forged above all in the convoluted twists and turns of his own nature and the circumstances of his life so far.

2

The Teacher of Prayer 1924–31

The Burgh

St Paul's Missionary College was situated in the tiny village of Burgh-le-Marsh on the edge of the Lincolnshire Wolds, a handful of miles from Skegness. It had been founded in the late 19th century with the specific intention of training priests to work abroad in the mission fields. Financial problems of various kinds dogged the life of the college from the beginning: being primarily concerned with sending its students abroad it was unable to draw financial support from the Church at home nor did its relative inaccessibility help draw men to it. The Principal already had to combine his work with that of a nearby benefice and it was made clear to Gilbert that he must include fund-raising among his activities. He came up with an imaginative scheme whereby ordinands would combine their study with work on local farms to the mutual benefit of college and community. Unfortunately the Church authorities were unconvinced that manual labour was appropriate for prospective clergymen and rejected the idea. It is not altogether surprising that the college was forced to close in 1936.

Throughout Gilbert's time there were about 35 students in residence at the college, amongst them Max Petitpierre who came at his suggestion. Most of them were studying for the General Ordination Examination though some went on to read for a L.Th by arrangement with the University of Durham. In addition to their theological teaching students were expected to play a full part in the domestic life of the college as well as gardening or involving themselves in the printing workshop and carpenter's shop which the college enjoyed. Staff, too, were expected to take their full share of the daily chores and Gilbert particularly enjoyed the carpentry he learned there, putting it to full use a decade later in Poplar. Students obtained their pastoral and liturgical experience from helping out in the many churches of Lincoln diocese.

Gilbert was the director of studies with regard to the spiritual life of the college. This was centred on the celebration of the daily office with fixed times for meditation as well as regular retreats. He was ever strong on the need for discipline and order in the life of prayer insisting that if you don't make time for prayer 'the devil will see you don't find it'. At times however his concept of discipline tended to get the better of him. For example, it is said that on one occasion he made a point of kneeling in prayer in the only college exit to the local pub at a time when he thought they should be praying and not drinking. To some people who knew Gilbert Shaw, this story, apocryphal or not, will merely serve to confirm their impression of him as an iron-willed and negative teacher, whose ministry seems to have been characterized by little joy and much of the *via negativa*. At certain stages in his ministry such an impression may well have been true. Indeed in his last days he asked that some of his papers and retreats from this period be destroyed because of their over-emphasis upon the negative way. On the other hand it is also clear that many people, far from being put off by his approach, were attracted by it and the numbers of people in the following years who found him helpful indicate that in some way he was ministering to a felt need. Thus, whilst it is necessary to maintain a sense of proportion about the *via negativa*, a spirituality shorn of discipline could never have sustained the sort of pressures and experiences which Gilbert was to encounter in the following years, nor can it today. Order and discipline continue to save us from the prison-house of self-absorption and forced spontaneity. Some of the students from his days at Burgh have confirmed that in the lonely outposts of mission in which they later found themselves it was only the hard discipline drilled into them by Gilbert that enabled them to survive. As he said to them on more than one occasion 'You are here to learn what holy ORDERS is all about'.

Gilbert himself took holy orders as a deacon in 1925 and in 1926 he was ordained priest in Lincoln Cathedral, shortly before his 40th birthday. If he made great demands on others as they prepared for ordination he certainly made no less upon himself but it was for him a moment of great joy and his friend Fr William of Glasshampton was among those who shared his delight. His ordination also marks the time when some of his writings on prayer began to be more widely known.

Affective prayer

The 1920s witnessed a great post-war flowering of interest in spirituality. Dom Cuthbert Butler, Abbot of Downside, a Roman Catholic Benedictine monastery, and a former Anglican published his important work *Western Mysticism*; the Anglican lay woman Evelyn Underhill in addition to her own many works on prayer and mysticism produced editions of classics of the English tradition of spirituality such as Walter Hilton's *Scale of Perfection* and *The Cloud of Unknowing*; in 1928 another Benedictine from Downside, Dom David Knowles, later to be Regius Professor of Modern History in the University of Cambridge, produced his book *English Mystics* which introduced many people to the works of Richard Rolle and Julian of Norwich. It was also a time of great spiritual directors: men such as the Baron von Hugel and Dom John Chapman among the Roman Catholics, Fr Andrew SDC and Evelyn Underhill herself for the Anglicans. Within a short time Gilbert Shaw was to be numbered among them. Indeed by 1932 when F.P. Harton (later Dean of Wells and for many years a good friend to Gilbert) produced his monumental work *The Elements of the Spiritual Life*, his reputation was such that he was almost alone among contemporary teachers and writers cited by the author in the body of the book.

His earliest efforts bore the modest title 'Burgh Booklets' and were drawn up initially for the students and then made more widely available. In 1927 Mowbrays published some similar material of his called *Prayers and Meditations for Lovers of Jesus*, which together with other writings from these years were later bound together as *A Pilgrim's Book of Prayers.*

Throughout his entire ministry as a teacher of prayer, Gilbert was at pains to stress that he was not an innovator but an expositor of the Church's tradition of mystical and ascetical theology and it seems a fair claim. In the 1920s there were few within the Church of England to whom this tradition was familiar. The majority of Anglo-Catholics were too engaged in controversies about what might be done in church, by whom, and wearing what, to give proper attention to providing more than basic spiritual instruction, to which their manuals of devotion with stylized 'methods' of meditation bear witness. Perhaps because Gilbert had never had a church building to occupy his attention such matters just passed him by and he had been able to explore the inner life of the Catholic faith. In the main this had come through his familiarity with the works of St John of the Cross, but he also had an extensive knowledge of the English tradition and made use of the works of the great 17th century writer Fr Augustine Baker.

He looked upon his early writings as something for the beginner in the life of prayer, to be closely allied to a regular discipline of some form of daily office and attendance at Mass. They were in the main exercises in prayer rather than theory about prayer, something for those who have already begun to use formal meditations, say of the Ignatian kind, and who have begun to feel the need to go deeper and largely do not know how. Within the Church's tradition of ascetical theology this was known as 'affective' prayer, although he had useful advice about definitions:

> People who use affective prayer, whether they know what they are using so that they can give it a name, or just happen to pray that way, had very much better not worry about its nature but should persevere in praying, leaving it to the Holy Spirit of God to lead them forward. There is a real danger that the soul should occupy itself in trying to estimate where it is or what it is doing on the ladder of prayer.

Gilbert himself was quite clear about where affective prayer fitted in the scheme of things. He understood it to be the next stage on from formal meditation towards contemplation in which the soul takes a phrase or perhaps just one word from the office or Mass and uses it to stir the affections Godwards. It is a way of controlling and directing the will, keeping the attention occupied as we wait upon God, and can be used either in a set period of quiet in which the phrase is slowly repeated or as what St Francis de Sales calls a 'bouquet' with which he could refresh himself during the day. It is taking prayer on from the discursive reasoning of meditation towards a more total response of the soul to God. Gilbert's earliest writings sought to provide examples of such prayer for people to use for themselves though he stressed that this sort of prayer also required reading and study to provide the material in the mind to fill out and enlarge, through the aid of the Holy Spirit, the particular thought which is held before the attention through repetition.

His writings from this period continue to be of value to many who pray and it is likely, with all the emphasis currently placed upon the rediscovery of Ignatian spirituality, that more people will need to know how to go on through the use of affective prayer. Although for those beginning to pray the use of formal 'methods' of meditation are invaluable, there also comes a time when many feel a strong need to go on and if there is no guidance available when people need help it may well be that they will give up instead. This was as much a concern for St John of the Cross as it was of Gilbert and will be equally appropriate now. There will be many who recognize something of themselves in the following passage given to a consideration of the use and value of repetition:

> There are many people who, with a real desire to pray, never bring any spiritual reality to birth in their souls because they turn themselves from book to book, from teacher to teacher, losing themselves in a multitude of different forms of words, spending time in saying many prayers, but praying little. A restless hen that frequently leaves the nest to find a better site, or spends much of her time rearranging her eggs will never hatch chicks; for only a quiet and persistent brooding will enable the dormant life to develop to the birth. In meditation we seek devotion; in affective prayer we find, and yet have to persevere in knocking, so that if the Master of life should of his will open the door of contemplative knowledge we are waiting on the threshold.

What appears to have communicated itself to those reading or listening to him was an impression that he spoke or wrote out of his own experience; not a knowledge about, but a knowledge of, God. He often spoke of foibles and weaknesses in people, knowledge of which could only have come from his own experience and this is what gives his writings a great deal of their power. Not that this makes them easy. He spoke of his earliest writings as being appropriate to the 'purgative' stage of prayer and if some readers find them unpalatable, perhaps they should see them as a reminder that whoever prays as a Christian does so only within the context of discipline and commitment. Throughout his entire ministry he was to stress that 'penitence' and 'dependence' were the hallmarks of prayer and must be implicit, if not actually expressed, in every expression of the soul's communication with God if it is to be preserved from becoming a subjective exercise in self-reflection or the expression of self-centred desire.

In his teaching Gilbert never attempted to cover up the difficulties of the spiritual life, the dryness, weariness or even desolation that besets men and women after they have made a beginning and which he also knew causes many of them to abandon it:

> Many fail by refusing to persevere in prayer and in their way of life when they seem to themselves unable to pray. They turn back to a dependence on worldly things and seek an outlet for their energies in a round of distractive occupations, interests. . . .
>
> Let the soul, then, that has been called away from the more discursive and exciting prayer of the mind to the simpler and shorter expression of the heart in the ways of affective devotion, have no fear when there is no feeling or taste in its devotional work. When prayer has become a labour, it is often more real, for it is then that the will by its perseverance and adherence to God in faith is able most perfectly to prove its devotion and express the disinterestedness of true love.

In his earliest teaching and writings Gilbert was above all concerned with this basic level of prayer whereby it moves from the mental towards the simplest experience of the contemplative. What he offers is an understanding and clear exposition of the basics of the life of prayer, an explanation not only of what happens when people pray but why things happen as they do as God leads them on. Most people, including priests, never advance beyond this so it is perhaps not surprising that many people responded to it for it seemed to speak directly to their condition. It is quite clear however that he himself was already further along the way and in later years as director of contemplatives, both within communities and 'in the world' was equally able to speak out of knowledge to their experience. Not that he would make any boast about being 'advanced' in prayer and indeed he once wrote that:

> 'Advance' in prayer, if this word is allowable, is not to be registered by any aptitude or facility in prayerful expression, but is more safely measured by the less obvious standards of detachment, unselfishness and a disciplined life.

No doubt he fell short in many ways, not least in an unhealthy over-emphasis upon mortification and penance, but his own life as a Christian already revealed, according to these standards, something of just how far he had advanced in the spiritual life, and which of course in turn equipped him to be of use to others.

From the first his writings were well received. The preface to the first edition of the Burgh Booklets was written by Jack Winslow, one of the first Christians to explore the interface of Christian and Hindu prayer, and he favourably compared Gilbert's writings to those of some of the best Hindu teachers. Among those helped by Gilbert's teachings were members of the Association for Promoting Retreats (APR), and from 1927 he was called upon to conduct a number of retreats for them, including some at Glastonbury. Out of these came a number of new booklets on prayer called 'The Glastonbury Series of Short Prayers', published by the

Church Union, whilst for the APR he produced some 'Introductory Notes to the Study of Devotional Literature'.

The Association for Promoting Retreats

Colleagues and students alike must have realized that his increasingly frequent excursions from college would eventually mean his permanent departure and it came to them as no surprize that at the end of 1927 he accepted the invitation of APR to become their full-time secretary, which work he began in the Spring of 1928. For the next three years from his office in Ecclestone Square he travelled throughout the country conducting retreats and quiet days, ministering to many who sought him out. In this period he built up a confessional of more than two thousand penitents, something surely without parallel within the Church of England, and perhaps only comparable to someone such as Fr John of Kronstadt, the 19th century Russian priest who served in the great naval port, and who like Gilbert was also a notable social campaigner.

His reputation quickly spread beyond Britain and in 1931, at the invitation of the well-known American spiritual writer Fr Shirley Hughson OHC, he toured the United States, conducting various retreats and lecturing to the College of Preachers in Washington. He also made use of the visit to see for himself something of the social effects of the economic collapse which had devastated parts of the country.

In spite of his apparent success, Gilbert was far from happy during his time with APR. In the first place, he found that there were many dangers in the whole concept of spiritual director, and although he may well have initially encouraged a spirit of dependence in those to whom he ministered he soon began to see how unhealthy that can become for both parties. It led him to be scornful in later years about certain trends in spiritual direction. He once said:

> There's only one director and that is the Holy Spirit. I'm a pilgrim sitting at the roadside on the way to Jerusalem and as the other pilgrims pass by I like to be able to give them a little word of encouragement to put them en route again.

Such an approach contrasted markedly with some of the pompous nonsense on the subject spoken by some of his contemporaries. The real value of Gilbert's words lay in the knowledge that this particular fellow-pilgrim knew the road ahead from his own journeys upon it. But he knew well enough that there were some clergy who wanted to set themselves up as directors of repute and who, it seemed to him, were manipulating their spiritual authority to serve their own ends, seemingly drawing a comfortable living from the practice. His knowledge of the experience of saints such as St John of the Cross or his personal contact with men such as Fr William made it clear to him that the mark of an authentic spiritual guide lay more in the direction of suffering than in the clamour of popular appeal. In all fairness however it would have to be conceded that in later years there would be those who laid similar charges against him, but if at times there was some truth in their complaints, he was always clear that such things were not right.

Another trend he disliked within APR was what he spoke of as its 'drawing room' mentality. It seemed to make prayer something reserved for relatively well-to-do ladies which had little to offer the people of Hackney or Camberwell. Many of those involved with APR seemd totally unaware of the severe economic slump going on about them, and those who did seemed to believe that the occasional sally into a soup-kitchen was an appropriate and morally upright response. Here too however Gilbert was not uncompromised and he maintained a love-hate relationship with some of the ladies of the APR for many years. He would often dismiss them as 'old pussies' from whose clutches he attempted to escape, whilst at other times he enjoyed their devoted attention, and in the course of the following years he was to turn to them for financial help on many occasions.

His other anxiety about APR was something that could never be laid against him however and concerned theology. From his earliest days at Burgh he had become aware of a widening gap between spirituality and theology. Theologians seemed less and less interested in prayer whilst those who prayed and taught prayer seemed sometimes far removed from the central doctrines of the faith. An example of this was Evelyn Underhill, the adulation for whose writings he largely did not share, for at times he believed her to be only vaguely Christian in what she wrote and taught. He was convinced that once dissociated from its theological roots, prayer could rapidly decline into one of those forms of syncretism or nature worship of which he knew from his study of the world of magic. The spiritual conflict, a major theme in his later writings, could not be taken seriously except from within the boundaries provided by the fulness of an orthodox theology. Arius could hardly have written the *Life of St Anthony*, but St Athanasius could and did.

Gilbert was aware that the absence of an adequate social and political awareness referred to above was equally a theological shortfall. He believed that the realities of poverty presented the Church with a fundamental challenge to its spiritual and theological integrity and he was rapidly discovering that in the face of it many of those who were devotees of the latest spiritual teaching were woefully inadequate. It troubled him that he was having to spend his time as a kind of 'chaplain' to such people, and by inference thereby condoning their untheological spirituality.

These anxieties pressed upon him throughout 1931 and he shared them with Fr William in the course of regular visits to Glasshampton. Fr William had now resigned himself to living as a solitary though in the manner of solitaries he nevertheless maintained a profound awareness of what was happening in the world beyond the confines of his hermitage. In part this was no doubt due to the fact that he was regularly visited by his near-neighbour Stanley Baldwin, whose confessor he was, but in the main it was because he retained his love for the people of the East End whom he had served as a friar. That love made him want to continue serving them, even from Worcestershire and so in 1930 and 1931 he and Gilbert organized conference–retreats at Glasshampton for priests from the East End. During the second of these, in which they were making a study of the Sermon on the Mount, they received word from Poplar that during a meeting concerned with unemployment, priests had been howled off the platform. This news served to enhance their view that increasingly the Church was being disregarded by the people of the East End. To those at Glasshampton the message came almost as a direct call from the Holy Spirit summoning them to a response though they seemed lost to know just what form it could take.

Gilbert's personal response to this retreat was a decision to resign immediately from APR even though he had no idea about alternative work. Temporarily he stood in as chaplain at St George's School, Ascot where his daughter Pat was a pupil, in the course of which he prepared her for confirmation, a process no doubt more substantial than he had known. Seeking longer-term guidance he went back to Glasshampton in the Spring of 1932 for a major retreat with Fr William which confirmed for him a growing sense that he was being called to make a personal commitment to work in the East End. Fr William concurred, although he would have very much liked to have gone himself had he not been persuaded that recent experience of ill health suggested such a course to be unwise. In the end, it was agreed that Gilbert would go as Fr William's emissary, to try and discover just what the Church might be able to do in the face of a mounting political and economic crisis. Both men felt that the crisis would reveal the need for the Church to be purged if ever it were to be renewed, and to the fore of Gilbert's mind as he set out were those words from the Epistle to the Hebrews which Figgis had loved to quote: 'Things are to be shaken, so that only the unshakeable will remain'.

3

'Christ in Chaos'
1932–40

With the unemployed

Arthur Winnington-Ingram had spent most of his ministry in London. He had once been Head of Oxford House in Bethnal Green, a centre in the East End for Christian social involvement; then he spent three years as Rector of Bethnal Green before, in 1897, being appointed Bishop of Stepney; four years later he became Bishop of London which position he held until 1939. Church historians have tended to see him in not too favourable a light mainly because of what has been considered to be an inappropriate jingoism during the first world war and perhaps their judgement has been somewhat over-harsh. He was a popular Bishop of London with the lay people of the diocese and he was never happier than when he had the chance to go back to his beloved East End where in earlier years he had enjoyed preaching to working men at open-air mission meetings.

In the early summer of 1932 Gilbert came to visit the Bishop in Fulham Palace. Almost twenty years earlier he had stood before him as a young and promising barrister and bridegroom. In the interim they had met on a number of occasions, Gilbert having been licensed to officiate in his diocese during his days with the APR. The Bishop also knew of Gilbert's reputation as a spiritual director. Now he stood before him seeking his blessing upon nothing more than a desire to be a Christian presence among the unemployed of the East End.

Although the idea of a Christian 'presence alongside the poor' sounds somewhat more familiar today, fifty years ago it must have struck the Bishop of London as most peculiar. Perhaps his previous knowledge of Gilbert's work gave him the confidence to support him in this new venture, or it may have been the fact that as Gilbert was not seeking an actual living it would not cost the diocese anything; either way the Bishop offered his support and gave his blessing.

Gilbert was licensed in a vague and unspecific way to the parish of All Saints, Poplar, but on arrival the incumbent made it clear that as far as he was concerned there was no question of his being regarded as a member of the staff of the Church. It was the first encounter in what was to prove an unhappy relationship between the two. Some other local clergy were similarly unwelcoming though a definite exception to this was Fr St John Groser, vicar of Christ Church, Stepney, with whom Gilbert became good friends. He was one of the great characters of the Church in the East End during the 1930s, a notable preacher who stood in a long line of fine Anglo-Catholic priests serving there since the 1880s.

At the heart of Gilbert's commitment lay the incarnational understanding of 'identification'. To this end he moved into a single room in the basement of a house owned by a retired priest, Fr Essex (who was the father of Rosamund Essex the journalist who for many years worked for the *Church Times*), and if he had ever wondered what he ought to be doing he didn't have long to wait in order to find out. In no time at all his room rapidly became full of boots, shoes and clothes, and a great number of men in need of them. Gilbert saw the provision of such basic needs as essential for men who often had to travel miles each day in search of work, and he put out appeals far and wide for shoes and boots. His basement room also served as a canteen in which basic food and drinks could be had by those in need. At night it often had to serve as a dormitory, with, in addition to Gilbert, four or five men sharing the floorspace. It didn't take him long to realize that much more needed to be done than was possible from this flat and he began to search for an alternative.

The solution surfaced in the form of some disused school rooms to which Gilbert brought groups of unemployed men whom he set to work cleaning and painting. He published an article about these rooms in the *Church Times*, which brought in over £100 in contributions and in January 1933 opened them as the Poplar Deanery Unemployed Centre. Before long the centre had a membership of more than two hundred. It had a canteen where cheap and nourishing food was available – three courses for fourpence halfpenny. Facilities were provided for carpentry, boot-repairing, physical recreation and reading. The day to day life of the centre was in the hands of a man who had himself been unemployed for more than five years, although the life of the place depended ultimately upon the initiatives and involvement of the members.

Until the opening of the centre, facilities for the unemployed were mostly non-existent and hanging about on street corners made them easy prey for the recruiting agents of the communists and fascists whose influence was growing. Their potential for trouble-making meant that membership of the Centre had to be tightly controlled. Even so, from time to time rival gangs managed to secure an entrance and more than once the police had to be brought in to restore order, though it was soon discovered that one of the most effective deterrents to trouble was the sight of the hefty Gilbert in his cassock standing in the doorway, as once he had blocked the exit of ordinands at Burgh.

Although Gilbert no longer practised at the Bar, his legal training did begin to come in useful when he represented families before the Public Assistance Committee and it was this work which began to make him realize the severe limitations of first-aid work and that what was needed instead was deep-rooted social change. The communists and fascists thought likewise of course, but he felt unable to ally himself with either party's manifesto for change and he was determined to find ways in which the Church could contribute something distinctive to the situation. From the beginning, however, he was determined that this must include neither using the Centre as a base for proselytism nor even for the holding of services. Perhaps in the end this manifests an approach which is distinctive: the expression of a practical love and concern which did not count the cost. It was a commitment to the one in need which asked nothing in return, neither some kind of 'decision for Christ' nor the signing of a party membership card.

The Sydney

The longer Gilbert remained, the more his work expanded and the more woefully inadequate became the room in Fr Essex' basement as a location for interviews. The Centre too was constantly overflowing with people and it rapidly became clear that new premises were necessary. The suggestion was put to Gilbert that he might be interested in a disused beer-hall called 'The Sydney' in Woolmore Street. As soon as he saw the place he recognized its potential but realized that it would cost more than he had available, so he wrote to as many of the 'old pussies' from the APR as he could and asked them for help. Within a short time they had provided the necessary funds and in May 1934 it opened. Gilbert was able to leave Fr Essex and move into a first floor room, which he had also fitted out with a darkroom for his photography. The ground floor area became the new Centre and the basement served as an excellent storeroom and carpentry shop.

'The Sydney' was run from day to day by Bill, an unemployed ex-police sergeant, who was also a Borough Councillor and who remained a great friend to Gilbert throughout his years in Poplar. The legal work of 'The Sydney' expanded that of the earlier centre and many local campaigns about housing or education were run from there. Gilbert was appalled to discover that of the four schools in the immediate area, three were little more than child-minding establishments and in one of which he discovered the head boy to be little more than illiterate. Whilst seeking to give as much time as he could to helping young people learn to read he also endeavoured to take any and every opportunity to draw public attention to the appalling state of affairs he was uncovering.

Foremost among the locations in which he sought to make known such things was The Athenaeum, a club in Pall Mall of which he was a life member. Here could be found many influential people in Church and State and Gilbert invited many fellow members to visit 'The Sydney'. Among those who took up his offer were Maurice Reckitt, the Christian social thinker who commented after his visit, 'We could do with a Sydney in every slum', the poet T.S. Eliot and Professor Bert Hodges, the Christian philosopher from the University of Reading who, together with his wife, became penitents of and close friends to Gilbert.

At this time Poplar Borough contained some 150–160,000 people, of whom twenty per cent were living below the official poverty level of basic subsistence and of the rest, the majority were living perilously close to it. As a result of a survey carried out by himself, Gilbert calculated that after making due allowance for heating, lighting, rent and washing, only fourpence halfpenny remained from the current dole payment per member of the family for a week's food. In such circumstances it is hardly surprising that there was considerable bad health among the population or that the perinatal mortality rate was so high. Inadequate food was also often allied to financial and legal difficulties. Many families found themselves defaulting in payments to money-lenders or hire-purchase companies and to help in these matters Gilbert instituted a 'poor man's lawyer' surgery at 'The Sydney'.

One of the major areas of Gilbert's involvement was that of housing. Housing stock was in an appalling condition, private landlords unscrupulous and overcrowding notorious. To help meet the needs occasioned by such factors Gilbert and Fr Groser set up a Tenant's Defence Association. In Poplar the Association took more than £2,000 off bad landlords and success was rapidly followed by an even greater demand for their services. Gilbert recalled that Association meetings at 'The Sydney' at times lasted as long as five hours.

The book edited by Brill on the life and work of Fr Groser suggested that it was he who initiated the work of the Associations. He was certainly President of the Stepney Association, but that was only one among others and Gilbert Shaw's legal experience lay behind the setting up of them all. Nor did Fr Groser play the leading role, as has been suggested, in the Hanbury Buildings rent strike of 1939. Tenants here had been unable to force their landlord to carry out necessary repairs and so with the backing of the Association, organized a rent strike. Contemporary newspaper reports make it abundantly clear that it was Gilbert together with a young social worker Jack Barker, who led the strike, and who after a two month long struggle secured a notable victory in the County Court. Barker commented that 'the high church Anglicans and the Communists were the only active people in the East End'; and with particular reference to the strike:

> To Hanbury Mansions came the Reverend Fr. Shaw to take charge of the strike. To him was owed the successful

outcome. His eloquence in the witness box in the case of the defaulting tenants undoubtedly swayed County Court Judge Thompson, who granted a stay of all rent due and for the following eighteen months.

It is clear that Gilbert's part in such activities was much appreciated by the people of Poplar, to which two much later events bear eloquent testimony. The first was the opening of a 'Fr Gilbert Playground' in Poplar in 1968 which was warmly welcomed by many who remembered him, and work upon the building of which had been done by among others, Michael Trend, Gilbert's grandson. The second was an exhibition mounted by the Greater London Council in the Royal Festival Hall in 1984 featuring various 'makers of modern history' in London, a stand being devoted to the part played by Gilbert in the rent strike of 1939.

Such popular acclaim was not always imitated by his fellow clergy, some of whom objected to his leading marches and demonstrations or being openly associated with communists, and who felt he ought to be more concerned with evangelism than good causes. Inevitably, landlords and money-lenders did not view him in too bright a light either. At one time a campaign was launched against him, whereby slogans were daubed all over the doors of 'The Sydney' though there was no shortage of men ready to defend him against any who might attempt a physical attack upon his person. The communists also had a deep respect for him, not least because he seemed to know so much about their position and views. The full extent of his knowledge only emerged in 1962 when as, librarian, Fr Donald Allchin was reorganizing the library at Pusey House, and Gilbert offered his books on Marxism. Fr Allchin accepted the offer but was astonished at the quantity and quality of the books brought by Gilbert. Clearly he had made as thorough a study of Marx and Communism as he had earlier studied magic and in Poplar he probably knew more about Marxism than any who actually called themselves Marxist.

It is important to set the activities of the likes of Gilbert and Fr Groser within a proper perspective. They would have been the first to acknowledge how little they actually achieved, but within the limited spheres of their activity they were undoubtedly major influences for good and at least helped to maintain the good name of the Church in some places. Affection for the Church was not high. On one occasion during a meeting in 'The Sydney', Gilbert made a passing reference to the Bishop of London. An unemployed man present commented that he thought people like that couldn't give two hoots for those like himself. To prove the contrary Gilbert arranged for the Bishop to receive a party of Poplar men for tea at Fulham Palace. The Bishop turned up trumps and having served almost the whole of his ministry before becoming Bishop in the East End, greatly enjoyed their company. On the journey home, the aforementioned unemployed fellow commented to Gilbert: 'You know, I feel bloody sorry for that nice old man. Fancy having to live in a big house like that'.

The Mission of the Church

In spite of the hostility engendered among some of them, Gilbert endeavoured to keep the clergy of Poplar in touch with his work and as far as possible to involve them. For this reason he had called the first unemployment centre, the 'Deanery' centre, to emphasize that it belonged to the whole Church. He also brought out a regular newsletter which he called *Poplar News* and in one particular article expressed the rationale for his work:

> The Christian religion is concerned with the whole life of man, the material things of life, food and clothing; the material social order in which the reign of righteousness must be established as well as the mental outlook and

> those things more specifically termed as religious, and until the Christian Church as a whole realises the importance of the material field of spiritual operation there can be no hope of revival. Without that return to the gospel in word and deed, religion remains at the best a thing of culture, at the worst a kind of aestheticism – an emotional satisfaction to the religious instinct, which is only worthy of the very just accusation of those who are against God, and who in derision call it 'dope'. In this mad world which is given up to selfishness and fear the earnest Christian must be occupied in protesting against the madness. The Christian has to protest against the lack of social righteousness whether it be in regard to the toleration of unemployment, underfeeding, over-working or under-educating.

Although he was criticized by some for being over concerned with social and political questions, the newsletters also reveal something of the direct mission work in which he was engaged. In fact he was quite clear that the work of 'The Sydney' and its predecessor in its provision of basic needs was 'only the first step towards the far more important work of evangelism . . . the work of compassion is an evidence of true religion, but it is not the preaching of the Good News.' Although, as has been mentioned, he did not allow the unemployment centres to be used for evangelism, he did himself engage in direct mission work, including open-air preaching.

Included in this mission work was the introduction of a special Mass at 9.30 am on Sundays at All Saints. The incumbent, Fr Maine, would not allow it to be advertized and expressed some anxiety about the sort of person who was coming to it, but Gilbert wanted it to be a service to which anyone would feel able to come, irrespective of dress. He simplified the liturgy and employed a portable nave altar because he thought these would help the congregation make more sense out of what was happening. Gilbert was and remained a totally committed catholic Anglican but could not stand a type of conservative catholicism which baulked at such changes. To the end of his life one of the phrases he reserved for certain priests was that so-and-so was 'a 1930s anglo-catholic', clearly a terrible indictment in his eyes. It would be surprizing if the origins of this were not be found in his experience of All Saints, Poplar.

At All Saints he also introduced a weekday afternoon service for mothers and babies and occasionally in the evening he would put on a magic lantern show. He had obtained a mighty brass projector, with which he showed scenes from the gospels in modern dress featuring photographs taken by himself, including one which showed the prodigal son returning home across Poplar Bridge.

In 1938 the Bishop asked him to take charge of the church of St Nicholas, Blackwall Stairs, a lofty red building only five minutes walk from 'The Sydney' and later, having been demolished by the Luftwaffe, to be replaced by the Blackwall Tunnel. Given the persistence of tension between himself and All Saints, Gilbert was glad to accept this new charge where he would have considerably more space in which to engage in mission work. He fitted the church out to cope with his audio-visual aids and had plans for a studio. The SPCK, hearing of his audio-visual work, invited him onto their Committee for Religious Films though he was largely unimpressed with the quality of what he saw.

Prophetic theology

The writings of the liberation theologians and the passage of time tend to obscure the innovatory nature of Gilbert's work in Poplar. There was already a significant tradition of Anglo-Catholic priests operating in the East End of which Fr Groser was a fine representative, but Gilbert was going somewhat further. In the first place he took the incarnational principle further, in that for most of his time he had no security – neither living nor stipend. He shared his own dwelling with others and they recognized him as one who lived as simply as themselves. Any priest who could at the end of the day retreat into a comfortable Vicarage was unable to share that.

Second, although no one was more willing than Gilbert to be involved in political and social issues, in his own mind and thus consequently underlying his whole work, lay the total conviction that primarily he was involved in something that was inherently spiritual. Of course for one so rooted in theological orthodoxy it was natural to recognize that any Christian living which claimed in some way an adherence to the incarnation meant that the material world is the medium of the spiritual but Gilbert developed this further. From his reading and conversations with Fr William, whom he continued to visit at Glasshampton, he was already developing his understanding of eschatology, that is, the relationship between the life of the world and the life of the Kingdom of God.

It was this line of thought that had first been opened up for Gilbert by Figgis thirty years earlier and which in one form or another was to predominate throughout his remaining work. Its starting point lay in the fact of the Church. In spite of its failures, it did not cease to be the Body of Christ and the question which had to be faced concerned the function of the Church in the East End. Was it to be just another social agency engaged in work alongside others, or did its particular identity make it something different, and if so, how and what?

It was abundantly clear, and this was spelled out in the article in *Poplar News* above, that the Church had to be clearly seen to care for people in practical terms, especially in the face of enormous need, and to do so without counting the cost of such a commitment. It was also certain that some needs were so urgent that meeting them must be a priority, and in this it was for the Church to set a clear example. Nor did this just mean first-aid, Gilbert knew that works of service and love would inevitably and justly take him into the realms of corporate and political action, though he was quite clear that the Church did not need and perhaps should not identify with any particular party, even though some would be more natural bed-fellows than others. It is when these things are being attended to and realized as part of the work of the Church alongside and with other agencies that the Church has to consider its own unique identity as the Body of Christ.

The point of departure in thinking about the identity of the Church has to be God. God has called the Church into being and continues to sustain it for the purpose of serving the Kingdom. The Kingdom of God is not something that merely belongs to the realm of the beyond, the after-life, but is also that which is constantly breaking into this world, drawing it to its completion, its fulfilment in Christ. Thus central to understanding the work of the Church lies the necessity of grasping the work of God in relation to the world. Put simply, what God is doing, the Church is called to assist or co-operate with and forward.

He did not baulk at publicly expressing his beliefs and in 1935, at a lunch hour service in Westminster, made a strong appeal for the Church to take seriously its own reports about the need for social action:

> There can be no peace in this war-shattered world until the causes of war are altered, until the national spirit is exorcised and we see ourselves as Christians first and British second, till we can think internationally, and can control finance, not for financiers, but for men and women. Likewise there can be no settled order of life, or social structure until the need of our brother in want is satisfied. Do not be misled. No temporary increase in

> employment will satisfy his need. For either some new catastrophe, some new financial panic, or a return of the cycle of trade will soon bring a new and deeper depression. The foundations of our society are at fault, for they are of gold not God. It is for us to follow boldly the lead of our Bishops in the Lambeth reports which set forth that 'it is an outstanding and pressing duty of the Church to convince its members of nothing less than a fundamental change in the spirit and working of our economic life'. The common people whom our Lord loved and whose simple reasoning is often nearer the truth than the sophisticated expressions of culture puts this more pungently in the one word REVOLUTION. This dying world needs one thing – a revolution to put God in the Centre of its social life, to proclaim again the living Gospel as good news to the poor and as having a living contact with every part of life. The solemn decisions of our Bishops mean nothing unless they are translated into action. It is a hollow mockery if we should quote from the same Lambeth Conference to show the mind of the Church such phrases as 'that for every men there must be sufficient to live a decent and complete, a cleanly and a noble life', and having quoted we should tolerate and continue to tolerate the present conditions and do nothing to protest against and alter them.
>
> As long as those statements stand merely in print and are unapplied in life the Church is in danger of apostasy, of sinning more deeply because she knows the truth and refuses to act.

Gilbert was also quite clear that God is not merely interested in repairing a broken social order. It was the brokenness of the world and the inevitable brokenness of all its social orders that led to the incarnation and the redemption, and God didn't become man to patch them up, but rather to bring them to their fulfilment in the Kingdom.

From time to time of course the healing of people and communities occur, instances when it is possible to suggest that the fulness of the life of the Kingdom breaks into the world, but such encounters are no more than a proleptic experience of fulfilment, and not the final experience itself. For that reason even Lazarus would die again. So although first-aid and healing are vital and important they are penultimate realities and not those which pertain to the fulness of the Kingdom.

Gilbert believed that it was the unique vocation of the Church to be participating in God's work of drawing the creation to its End. In the first place this is through her life of prayer and worship, both of which are, and especially in relation to the celebration of the Eucharist, the total proleptic participation in the fulness of the End which is Christ. Wherever these were celebrated and lived, the death and resurrection of Christ are truly re-presented, drawing the world to that completion of creation which they have embodied and enabled.

Second, and intimately related to the first, lies the recognition that the Church exists not just to contend with human injustices but with the 'principalities and powers, the world rulers of this present darkness, the spiritual hosts of wickedness in the heavenly places'. In other words, the Church knows itself caught up in spiritual conflict, a participant in the Lord's overcoming of evil. All human sin and injustice is ultimately rooted in the rebellion of the spiritual domain. Although it would be twenty years before Gilbert gained an adequate language in which to speak of these things, he knew that it meant a particular way of discipleship – of living in a particular way so as to be properly equipped for the combat of the conflict. And in holding together these two aspects of his experience of being the Church, there began to grow within him the recognition, with which he was to be concerned for the rest of his life, of the need for contemplatives in the world. A phrase, derived from Fr William, which expressed this was 'the charioteers and horsemen of the army of God'. Of course the whole Church was meant to be this, but there was the definite recognition that areas such as those in which he lived needed the presence and prayer of contemplatives, and they in turn would need priests and others to guide them adequately.

His own living embodied such things and his entire Poplar ministry cannot be understood aright unless it is seen as being rooted in Gilbert's own dedication to worship and the life of prayer. Each day began with the celebration of Mass and in addition to a considerable period of silent prayer there were either breaks for the Office of the Hours, or more often short acts of recollection, continuing as it were, the Mass throughout the entire day.

The third aspect of the Church's life drawn from its being in Christ, was the need for the proclamation of the word, making known the truth about what God has done and is doing, and by inference, therefore, what the Church is for, to a world which largely does not know. This work of evangelism in a variety of forms increasingly took up Gilbert's time in the later years of his time in Poplar.

There is no doubt that the time spent by Gilbert in the East End was immensely rich. Many of his most important insights about the life of the Church and its place in the world which were eventually distilled into the teachings given to the sisters at Fairacres thirty years later were drawn from this experience and from reflection upon it. It also marks the beginning of his concern for those living as contemplatives in the world as well as his often fruitless search for those able to guide them.

Clearly a most important feature of this period was the opportunity he had to share his experience and to reflect upon it with Fr William, whom Gilbert continued to visit in Glasshampton until, in 1936, illness meant he had to move to the home for aged clergy at Lingfield. Gilbert believed that he and Fr William were partners in the work done in the East End, and would never have accepted that he was doing more by his presence in Poplar than Fr William had done through his intercession in Worcestershire.

Although Fr William had known no apparent success in his attempt to establish the contemplative life for men, neither had he lost his belief that he was a herald of that life within the Church of England. As his confessor and director Gilbert shared the conviction. It is therefore not unimportant to note that in 1938, shortly after Fr William's death, just a handful of miles away in a small wood near the village of Crawley Down, Gilbert helped a priest whom he knew from London, Fr Robert Gofton-Salmond, to purchase some land on which was established a religious community which has subsequently flowered into precisely that contemplative community of men for which Fr William had hoped.

The coming of war brought his Poplar ministry to a close. St Nicholas church was destroyed and the unemployment which had brought him to the East End had all but disappeared; there now seemed nothing to keep him there and although not everyone understood his decision to leave, he left at the beginning of 1940 and went to join Sylvia at Wallingford where she was living.

There have been those who have argued that his Poplar years were his happiest. The photographs from the period certainly manifest a well-being which was later to evade him for more than 20 years. He clearly enjoyed being with the people of the East End but it ought not be lost sight of that above all else he believed he was there in response to a definite call to participate in one aspect of the spiritual conflict, that which he expressed by the phrase 'Christ in chaos redeeming the world to himself'. It was only in the strength provided by such a faith that any of his work had been possible.

In his recent book *Spirituality and Pastoral Care* Fr Kenneth Leech has outlined six elements that he regards as hallmarks of a ministry that may be called 'prophetic'. First, he notes that prophets have been men of vision, 'seers'. Second, that this vision was linked to contemplation, they were men of profound prayer. Third, that before engaging in their ministry they came to know the context of their work intimately. Fourth, that ministry is exercised from within situations which demand discernment and does not consist of pronouncements made from outside. Fifth, that there is often a somewhat eccentric side to their nature. Sixth, that they were above all intensely human people whose concern is with the whole of life and not just religion. By these criteria there can be no doubt that it is not inappropriate to speak of Gilbert's time in Poplar as prophetic. He had been brought there by his vision and was sustained by his prayer. He fully entered into the realities of social life and where he needed knowledge he sought it himself and it was from within that he spoke to the circumstances of life. His lifestyle was considered odd and not without risk but the insecurity of his living was an enormous strength in ministering to those who also lived insecure lives. Finally he was a man who knew full well that before anything else and certainly before religion, men and women need food and clothing.

Perhaps a final mark of such a prophetic ministry is that many years after, his life and work continue to say something positive and important to the Church about how it is to relate to the world and its needs, and perhaps also how it can continue to speak about God in all those contexts, many of them not dissimilar from those with which he was dealing, in which ministry is to be exercised.

4

Trial and Errors'
1940–47

The Moot

Gilbert's decision to go and live with Sylvia in Wallingford was made on pragmatic grounds rather than on a desire to set up home again with his wife. They had continued to see each other throughout the Poplar years for he had tried to visit her most weeks if possible though their relationship was very strained. Now they were sharing the same house again, tension between them was often great. But in practice Gilbert had little alternative and after the East End a house in the country with its extensive orchard and fine gardens was something that brought him great delight. He discovered that he had something of a penchant for landscape gardening (some of his designs still remain at Fairacres) and he greatly enjoyed the opportunity for doing necessary work in the orchard.

In the meantime he set about collating his writings on affective prayer preparatory to their publication in 1945 and continued his work as a spiritual director. He also began to hold a series of conferences, which were to continue for a good number of years, in which he could develop his concern for contemplatives living in the world. He knew that there were many such, who with the right training and direction could exercise considerable ministries through their life and prayer. The problem lay in finding priests of the necessary calibre to direct them. In the remaining twenty-seven years of his life, during which time this concern for contemplatives living in the world was ever to the fore, he found very few such priests.

Although he was glad to enjoy a time of rest at Wallingford he had no wish to return to agriculture for a living and to the fore of his mind was a concern as to what he should now be doing. He no longer had Fr William to advise him and it seems that he decided to wait for definite guidance to come to him rather than setting out to find it. He was now fifty-four years old and in many ways might realistically have expected some preferment or other to come his way for his work in Poplar had brought him a fair amount of attention and acclaim and if it didn't bring him the instantaneous offer of work he was seeking, it did provide a number of important openings.

The first followed on from the Oxford international conference on 'Church, Community and State' in 1937, an event which was to prove a major watershed in Christian social thinking. The conference was the brainchild of Dr J.H. Oldham, a Scottish layman of enormous importance in the history of the Church in this century. A man of enormous vision and a founding father of the modern ecumenical movement, he had long been involved in seeking to face social problems in the light of Christian faith. After meeting Gilbert at The Athenaeum he had visited 'The Sydney' and was impressed by what he saw, recognizing it as an initiative of singular importance in the Church's concern for the unemployed. Although he had been unable to persuade Gilbert to take part in the Oxford conference, Oldham was determined that he should somehow be involved in the follow-up.

Oldham had begun to see more clearly than many others, that at the heart of Europe lay an ideological gap and the tensions engendered by this were tearing apart the traditional democratic nations. Fascists and communists were vying with one another for the chance to bridge this gap. Oldham wanted a new social programme or creed, to which say, the people of Britain, could commit themselves, as an alternative to those of the totalitarians. To this end he was responsible for three initiatives. The first was a regular publication, *The Christian News-Letter*, which was to be highly influential in the immediate post-war period; the second initiative set up a body called the Christian Frontier Council, which concerned itself with industrial and economic matters as a kind of 'think-tank'; the third, the one in which Gilbert was to be involved, was the bringing together of an élite group of thinkers who could serve as a kind of moral and intellectual backbone to the other initiatives.

This group which first met in 1938 was known as 'The Moot', and came together in a country house for a weekend at quarterly intervals throughout the following nine years. Oldham had a genius for cross-fertilizing minds from diverse backgrounds and this was reflected in the membership. In addition to Gilbert Shaw and Oldham himself, the regular members included T.S. Eliot, the Scottish theologian Prof. John Baillie, the educationalist Fred Clarke, the Revd Eric Fenn from the BBC who acted as unofficial secretary, the philosopher Prof. Bert Hodges from Reading, the eminent sociologist Karl Mannheim, the distinguished Christian thinkers Sir Walter Moberley and John Middleton Murry, and the Revd Alec Vidler, later to be Dean of King's College, Cambridge. Occasional visitors included men such as the philosopher Michael Polanyi, the influential American social writer Reinhold Niebuhr, Professor R.H. Tawney and the young Lesslie Newbigin.

All meetings were in private and only the minimum of records kept. Papers were prepared in advance, circulated and read. In September 1939, Mannheim, Moberley and Gilbert met together in London and drew up the nearest attempt ever made at a definition of what the Moot was:

> Membership. The Moot is a body of friends who have established through a common experience a certain relationship and corporate life which they desire to preserve unimpaired, therefore the relationship should be strictly limited to the original group and new members should only be introduced in small numbers. The total membership of the Moot should never be larger than a number which allows of free and intimate discussions.

A predominantly lay group, its concerns were for the development of society in the years after the war and the intellectual foundation of what was subsequently to be the pattern of the democratic socialism which characterized British life from 1945. Most of its really useful work was done prior to 1940 and too easily did it become little more than a 'talking shop' for fashionable social ideas. In the end its chief value seems to have lain in the intellectual comradeship it provided for members and was clearly a source of disappointment to Oldham. In the course of time his role as convenor diminished and Karl Mannheim emerged as the leading light, so much so, that after his death in 1947 the group never met again.

Gilbert attended most meetings up to 1945. Oldham had wanted him as a member because of his experience in Poplar but the prevailing intellectual climate of meetings was much more concerned with social theory than practical consequences. Apparently some of the members saw him as a somewhat mysterious figure and uncharacteristically he spoke little and when he did it seems that few members understood him. To them he appeared to be endeavouring to unite science, politics and theology in a way that mostly left them baffled and it may well be that in such company he was out of his intellectual depth. Most of the membership had been drawn from academic institutions and were much more used than he to the rigours of what he sometimes felt was just a verbal game. On the other hand his approach to social matters was quite different from theirs. None of them had his practical experience nor did they share his particular theological perspective which may well account for their finding him unintelligible. He was honoured to be numbered among such men but retrospectively was very unhappy about what he saw as the uncritical liberalism of the group. He was moving in quite a different direction by 1945.

Among others impressed by Gilbert and his work in Poplar were members of the Industrial Christian Fellowship who invited him to join their Council. It was no longer the influential body it had been in the immediate post-war period when Geoffrey Studdert-Kennedy had been its leading light but had yet to be eclipsed by the rise of Industrial Mission. They had published occasional papers written by him on social matters during the 1930s and at the initiative of the director, Preb. P.T.R. Kirk, Gilbert was made responsible for arranging a major conference at the Royal Albert Hall in September 1942 'The Church Looks Forward'. Speakers included both Archbishops, the Bishop of Bristol and the Lord Privy Seal, Sir Stafford Cripps, and was in part an attempt by the churches to begin planning for the immediate post-war period.

The growing menace of war throughout the late 1930s found Gilbert among the ranks of Christian pacifists. John Middleton Murry whom he knew from the Moot, persuaded him to write the occasional article for *Peace News*, of which he was editor, and during the war he was a contributor to two major works expounding the position of Christian pacifism edited by Percy Harthill, Archdeacon of Stoke-on-Trent, who had founded the Anglican Pacifist Fellowship in 1937. It seems somehow contradictory that a man such as Gilbert Shaw should have felt disposed to espouse the pacifist cause in the face of Hitler when, as we shall see, he was in other contexts so determined to resist and destroy evil in its supernatural forms. It seems equally peculiar that he should reject the liberalism of the Moot whilst identifying himself with such thoroughgoing liberals as Charles Raven or Leslie Weatherhead. That he himself recognized a certain tension about this emerges from his contributions to the Harthill books. Moot members reading them would at once have recognized that apparently confusing amalgam of theology, politics and eschatology they had come to associate with Gilbert. More than forty years on it is not always easy to tell from reading them whether he was in fact for pacifism or against it.

These involvements of the early war years, arising out of his work in Poplar, presented Gilbert with important opportunities which somehow he failed to make full use of. This cannot be accounted for just in terms of the vagaries of his nature; it was much more that he was developing in quite a different sort of direction from that which was becoming predominant among church leaders. No more was this revealed than in the circumstances surrounding the work which was eventually offered him in 1942 by Dr Geoffrey Fisher, then Bishop of London.

St Anne's, Soho

His new work was to be based in Soho where he was invited to become warden of the St Anne's Centre with the aim of ministering to the intelligentsia of London. St Anne's Church had been bombed but the adjoining church house was intact and this was to be linked up with the parish of St Thomas, Regent St. and Toc H in Westminster for the new work with a team which would also include a Deaconess Hunter, the Revd Patrick McLaughlin and Gilbert's old friend Max Petitpierre. Having waited for guidance this seemed to provide it and he accepted at once. The house opened in 1943 as a Centre for 'Christian discourse', with the aim that it should provide men and women with opportunities for considering the relationship of the Christian faith to contemporary culture. An initial series of lectures included among its speakers T.S. Eliot, Dorothy L. Sayers and Sir Eric Maclaglan, the director of the Victoria and Albert Museum. In addition to the programme of lectures there were discussion groups, one of which was led by Gilbert and included Dorothy Sayers. Although she thought him 'saintly', she confessed to a friend that she found him 'quite unintelligible'. Clearly this inability to communicate was becoming a problem and it rapidly assumed major proportions at St Anne's, where presumably, communication was of the essence.

It seems likely that none of Gilbert's time at St Anne's was particularly happy. From the beginning there was a significant conflict of interests between he and McLaughlin. Gilbert wanted worship, prayer and the development of contemplatives to be the major thrust of the work whilst McLaughlin wanted a greater emphasis upon the intellectual aspect, in which respect he was undoubtedly more in line with the initial intentions of those who had set up the Centre. There was also a clash of personalities; Gilbert was not really a team man and was only really happy when he had a completely free hand to direct things as he himself saw fit, which when allied to his habit of speaking at people, as if giving them a lecture with apparent disregard for what they might be contributing, served to make him a difficult colleague. Reports of such difficulties became known and no matter how great had been the respect he had formerly earned, he was now rapidly acquiring quite a different reputation.

Gilbert had been appointed on the basis of what Fisher and others assumed about him because of his work in Poplar. In fact Gilbert was never the person they took him to be, nor clearly did they really understand the rationale which underlay his work in the East End. They supposed that he had changed from the man whose work they had so admired, but all along he had been much more concerned with spirituality and the life of prayer than with the sort of intellectualizing of faith that he had encountered in the Moot and which he was now expected to direct. Not only that, but the direction in which his theological understanding was developing, not least in response to some of the discoveries he was making in relation to the occult (which will be considered in the following chapter), was making him increasingly suspicious of any theology which he believed accommodated itself to the patterns of prevailing secular thought.

The conflicts at St Anne's came to a head over the use put to the chapel, a room adjoining Gilbert's own in the basement. McLaughlin wanted to turn it into a coffee lounge and move the chapel to a smaller location upstairs. In Gilbert's mind such a move assumed major proportions, the suggestion representing all that he held to be wrong with the priorities of the Centre and he used the incident as the occasion upon which to tender his resignation to William Wand, the new Bishop of London.

The incident provoked an enormous amount of bad feeling and Gilbert must have realized that his resignation would be held against him. He became aware on visits to the Athenaeum that some of the Bishops he met there increasingly looked upon him as something of a dangerous eccentric who practised an unhealthy asceticism, a reputation which was made even worse by rumours of his involvement with the occult and exorcism. Now almost sixty, Gilbert was heading into some kind of exile, but an exile demanded by the logic of his theological and spiritual commitment. Within the Church of England theological liberalism was in the ascendancy, in part a reflection of the optimism which seemed to dominate the nation as a whole in the earliest years of post-war euphoria. The development of the World Council of

Churches, a spiritual counterpart of the United Nations and at first primarily a gathering of liberal Protestant churches, set the tone for Church life and senior appointments noticeably reflected this trend. Such a mood ran quite counter to what was happening within Gilbert Shaw and if just a few years earlier he had been thought to embody all that was good in the Church, from now on he would be viewed with the gravest suspicion.

After his departure the St Anne's Centre continued to operate under the direction of McLaughlin, the tenor of the programmes organized by him being increasingly dominated by cultural rather than theological activities. Deaconess Hunter continued to work there but Petitpierre left in 1947 to join the monastic community at Nashdom. The Centre finally closed when McLaughlin left the Church of England in the mid-fifties to become a Roman Catholic.

St Alphege, Southwark

The decision to leave St Anne's deprived Gilbert of a formal reason for remaining in London. Nevertheless he decided that there were good reasons why he should try and find somewhere to live in the capital. In the first place it remained the ideal base for travelling to conduct missions and retreats. Second he had once again run up a significant confessional and was still hoping to train men and women to live as contemplatives in the world; to move back to Wallingford would have necessitated running down most of this work. So, early in 1946 he moved from Soho across the river, accepting an invitation from Fr Freddie Gain, vicar of St Alphege, Southwark to join him in the clergy house of the parish. This provided Gilbert with both a spiritual base and also a fairly central location for his work. Fr Percy Coleman, then secretary of the Church Union also lived at St Alphege's in a small flat annexed to the church hall and he was astonished to find what had formerly been his vicar's study now transformed by Gilbert into something resembling a cross between a woodshed and a bedroom. Gilbert had brought up from Wallingford sufficient wood to last him a year which he stored in his room with his books and simple camp bed.

Gilbert was to be based in Southwark for the next seventeen years and it was a pretty basic, if not austere, existence that he eked out for himself. Visitors never saw him eat much more than apples and cheese, although if he ever felt in dire need of food he would make for the Athenaeum. He travelled a great deal and was often away at weekends but parishioners saw him during the week, though they tended to avoid his weekday Mass because it lasted so long. An ordinary low Mass, without music or a homily, could last one and a half hours, so taken up in prayer did he often become in the course of it, something which was to get worse, or better, as he got older. Fr Gain once reported that on All Soul's Day it was more than he could manage to get Gilbert away from the altar. More often than not, Gilbert's only congregation would be Miss Francesca Morcom, a penitent and devotee who acted as his secretary throughout his time in Southwark. Although she possessed undoubted spiritual gifts perhaps her most important talent was an unfailing ability to transform Gilbert's largely undecipherable squiggles into readable English, which she always typed up in green.

Gilbert often described the masters of the spiritual life as 'those who spoke out of knowledge'; he too spoke out of the knowledge fashioned by hours of prayer each day. On occasions there were reports of parishioners being terrified at the discovery of his prostrate body at prayer in the half-light of the church. Such stories may have puzzled them but they left no room for doubts about his priorities.

From 1945 Gilbert had a formal link with the women's Community of the Holy Name at Malvern as one of their visiting confessors and he also acted as confessor to a number of other religious. Most of his retreat work was now limited to clergy or religious communities, though the publication in 1945 of *A Pilgrim's Book of Prayers* had brought him many more people seeking spiritual guidance. Although he practised a rigorous asceticism and constantly stressed to others the cost demanded by the life of prayer he was by all accounts a most gentle confessor. Ever ready to reassure and mindful of the forgiveness which lies at the heart of the sacrament, he nevertheless asked one penitent as a penance, to learn the office of Compline by heart. Many of his penitents remained with him for years and there can have been few more experienced confessors. Yet he has left next to nothing in the way of teaching about the confessional. If there is a reason for this then it lies in the fact that he believed confession to be the Church's sacrament of forgiveness and not a method of psychological introspection. He assumed confession to be normative for anyone serious about the spiritual life, beyond which there seemed little worth saying. He was well aware that even penitence can become another opportunity for self-aggrandizement, another means of expressing self-interest. Instead of an obsession with failure he recommended a straightforward 'Sorry Lord, failed again; help me to do better next time', as the response to an occasion of sin, on the grounds that what matters is the turning back to Christ and not the spiritual navel-gazing of some penitents and too many confessors.

As gentle as he was in the confessional, formidable could he be in the retreat house. Retreatants had to expect two addresses per day of up to one and a half hours duration and often delivered at breakneck speed. Those endeavouring to take notes were often forced to abandon the exercise by the sheer overwhelming speed and duration of an address. He could on occasion however be persuaded to leave the text at the back of the chapel for later perusal, otherwise it was a matter of gleaning what one could out of the manifold riches presented before them. Compensation for retreatants lay in the opportunity for a private interview with him, and despite the manner in which he gave retreats, many priests returned again and again.

The content of retreats after 1945 was largely related to prayer within the traditional pattern of 'purgative : illuminative : unitive'; not a matter of techniques, nor a question of various levels to be striven for, but an attempt to give expression and form to hundreds of years of experience. In this respect his teaching remains contemporary. Aspects of it, such as the use of penance and the discipline may well require some modification, but even these, the significance of which has largely been lost, surely have some place within the life of prayer.

Gilbert was seeking to set out the basic foundations of prayer within the Christian community. Central to this was the need for those who pray to have a 'rule', a pattern of discipline in order to sustain and support them. He drew up a basic outline of such for those seeking to live as contemplatives, largely based upon his own experience of living the life of prayer in Poplar. Its foundations lay in the Eucharist as the focus of unity and the Divine Office as the means of continuing the action of the Eucharist throughout the day. Considerable provision was also made for solitary prayer, spiritual reading and an annual retreat. He was careful however to ensure that what was being undertaken was not a lifeless formalism but a life of conformity to the demands of the gospel and an intimate relationship with the Father, and it was made clear that such a rule should only be drawn up and lived under supervision.

In 1947 Gilbert was invited to become Chairman of G.J. Palmer & Sons, the parent company of *The Church Times*, in which capacity he acted until 1953. At first the arrangement was quite satisfactory, but gradually the relationship between members of the Board began to break

Joseph Shaw QC.

Charlotte Blanche Shaw at the time of their marriage.

Gilbert at Eton.

Gilbert the Undergraduate.

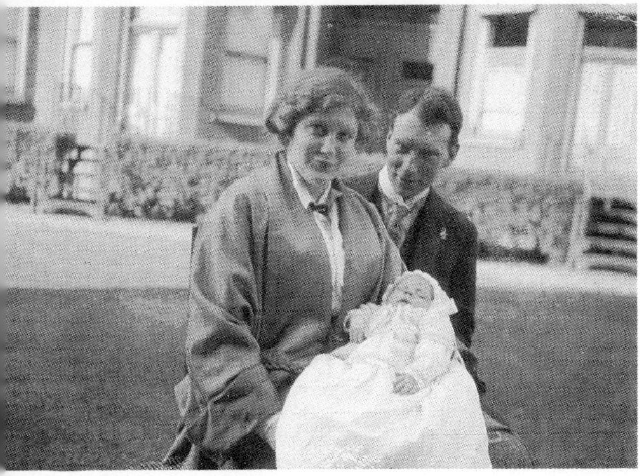

Gilbert, Sylvia and baby John.

Gilbert at 'The Sydney'.

Gilbert in Oxford.

down, most of the responsibility for which must lie with Gilbert. In some ways it was a repetition of the events at St Anne's. Gilbert wanted a greater involvement in editorial decisions and his typically forthright and robust manner was quite incapable or unwilling to recognize other viewpoints. As at St Anne's his approach was taken to be another manifestation of an arrogance which served to repel many of those whose only dealings with him were in these official capacities. The whole relationship between Gilbert and the company ended amidst much acrimony, although in 1963 Gilbert was touched to be invited back to the centenary celebrations of the newspaper, and there was no lasting bad feeling on his part about the way events had turned out.

It is clear that events such as those at *The Church Times* and Soho brought Gilbert into disrepute with many in the Church and inevitably this heightened within him a sense of isolation and even rejection. He was now entering the darkest period of his life, a time when it began to occur to him that he might not now be able to do justice to his deepest concerns about the place and training of men and women to live as contemplatives. But this falling darkness was now to be hastened by a considerable growth in the work he was now being called upon to exercise in relation to what he believed were the 'powers of darkness'.

5

The Darkness Deepens 1947–57

Involvement with the occult

In the years after his departure from Soho Gilbert Shaw had a considerable involvement in matters pertaining to the occult and the paranormal. He had been increasing this involvement for some years, not least through one particular case brought to his attention in 1929 and which occupied him until 1951. Before giving an account of such matters there are three important preliminary points which the reader should bear in mind in considering them.

The first derives from the notorious difficulties associated with any discussion of the paranormal because of the relationship between experience and theory. In the present context this refers to the fact that those who claim to be 'psychic' (and just what this might mean will be considered below) contend that this gives them an awareness of a reality inaccessible to those not similarly gifted. The effect of this contention can be to disallow or severely restrain critical consideration of truth-claims.

An equal restraint upon free consideration of these matters is derived from their 'spiritual' nature. Echoing those of earlier ages Gilbert was himself at great pains to stress that involvement was to be limited to only those with spiritual maturity and the appropriate gifts of discernment. Although he believed that all priests should know something about such things at the theoretical level, he was clear that no more than one or two ought ever to be involved practically, and that the first of all qualifications for such would be depth and maturity in the spiritual life. In effect this is saying, 'How can you expect those who are not living the spiritual conflict to understand it?'

In both instances we are presented with a realm of human life which, it is being maintained, only some can adequately recognize. If this was to avoid being turned into a case of the 'Emperor's new clothes' Gilbert knew that he had to set out as objectively as possible the rationale of his work and check it out with others, for which purpose he made use of Prof. Hodges and Dr Mascall. Neither of them made any claim to be psychic, but they were at least able to confirm that what Gilbert was discovering and discussing made logical sense within the boundaries of theological and philosophical discourse although they could not of course verify any particular truth-claims. It may be that the present intellectual climate is more open to accepting the possibility of the psychic, but there remains a great deal of confusion about how it relates to the spiritual. For that reason Gilbert's work and writings have by no means been superseded and remain significant for Christian involvement in such matters.

The second preliminary point is a warning about undue curiosity with regard to some of the matters to be considered. In a paper given to clergy in the diocese of Lampeter in 1947 he wrote:

> . . . we pray 'lead us not into temptation'. Curiosity and credulity because a subject appeals to the natural instincts as being exciting or uncanny, is entirely out of place. . . . It will help us to approach the subject to possess not only the detachment of religion but also the detachment of the scientific temper which will ruthlessly tear down the barriers of illusions and suggestions behind which the father of lies would work his evil and preserve his kingdom of discordance.

He concluded the same lecture by reminding those present that they should not go looking to be involved in such things: 'if it is the will of God that you should be concerned He will bring it to you. More than one person has been broken because they have ignored this simple maxim of humility'. Such an injunction applies in every age and echoes the warning of C.S. Lewis in the Preface to his *Screwtape Letters:*

> There are two equal and opposite errors into which our race can fall about the devils. One is to disbelieve in their existence. The other is to believe, and to feel an excessive and unhealthy interest in them. . . . Readers are advised to remember that the devil is a liar.'

Although Gilbert might have had some reservations about the first of these comments he profoundly agreed with the second and in time he would have sufficient evidence of its veracity.

The third point to be borne in mind is that the work of this period needs to be set in the context of his own spiritual development. All who pray, and especially those who persevere in the spiritual life, know times of darkness. After St John of the Cross these various experiences of darkness have been known as 'nights'. Initially, in the dark night of the senses the experience is one of dryness or disinclination and many never manage the necessary mortification and persistence required to get beyond it. At the first testing they abandon prayer. For those who do persist other nights follow, each in some way darker than the preceding, but all so that the soul can be that much more prepared for union with God. These nights can be long and their effects are not limited to some realm known as the 'spiritual'. Whereas the earliest experiences of dryness are usually during our times of prayer, the later darknesses cannot be so limited. St John of the Cross himself experienced the depths of night in the midst of his years of suffering and imprisonment. Outward and inward circumstances come together, and of this passive night of the spirit St John writes:

> . . . the soul seems literally to suffer the pains of hell . . . and to have its purgatory in this life; for this is the purgation which would have been endured there. Thus the soul which passes through this state in the present life, either enters not into purgatory, or is detained there but a moment, for one hour here is of greater profit than many there.
>
> The afflictions and distress of the will are also very great; they occasionally pierce the soul with a sudden recollection of the evils that environ it, and of the uncertainty of relief. . . . It also has the same sense of abandonment with respect to all creatures, and that it is an object of contempt to all, especially to its friends. (*The Dark Night of the Soul*)

Such teaching was well known to Gilbert, not merely in history, but also in his experience of men such as Fr William or some of the contemplatives to whom he ministered both in and out of religious communities. As he persisted in the life of prayer he must have known that some such experience would one day be his own. The decade from 1947 was to be the time of his own deepest testing, a time of prolonged night, both within and without. Of the internal night we have only the later fruits as they emerged into the greater light of his final years of teaching, but the fact of this inner darkness should not be overlooked as the encounters of the outer darkness are described.

The early encounter with Aleister Crowley and his experience at Eynsham had already alerted him to the dangerous nature of the world of the occult and by 1947 he already had more experience in such things than do most priests in a lifetime. It was in 1929 whilst he was with the APR that the most important development in his own involvement had occurred. A young girl was referred to him, through whom he came to know about the work of a group known as the Satanist Society. It had come into being in the early days of the French Revolution, when a number of apostate priests from France and Italy had combined a number of existing occult groups. The new society spread rapidly throughout Europe, entering England in 1830 and by the end of the century had an International Council which brought together learning from cultic traditions as diverse as the Voodoo, Dervish and Kali sects of India.

It was a lifelong boast of Crowley that he was a great master of the black arts. Gilbert discovered that this was not so but that there was at least one genuine Grand Master in England from 1924. Italian by birth, he had once been a priest, who after an overt moral lapse was defrocked and then excommunicated for having dabbled in magic. He left Italy, travelling through central and eastern Africa in an effort to learn more about magic and the occult. After some time in Egypt he travelled to India where his natural gifts were recognized by members of the society who initiated him into membership. It was from here that he came as a master magician to England together with three Indian helpers.

The girl (whom for convenience will be called Pauline) brought to Gilbert had come under the influence of this particular man at the age of twelve. Her mother had been an adherent of Crowley and it is believed that Crowley had dedicated her as a baby to the service of the black arts. Pauline was undoubtedly possessed of unusual psychic and telepathic gifts and under hypnosis had been brought under the total control of the Italian. None of this was apparent to Gilbert when they first met. Some friends of hers had heard that he sometimes spoke of the reality and dangers of the occult and brought her to him because of the bizarre behaviour she sometimes manifested. She lived in the East End of London and, although he did not know it at the time, within three years he would be living close enough to be able to keep a careful watch upon her.

Gilbert's first response was to seek medical and psychological help for her. Her doctors were unable to discover anything which they could pin-point though one of those consulted by Gilbert did confirm that she seemed to have an unusual degree of psychic sensitivity. It was only when praying about her that Gilbert began to be aware of the nature and extent of that with which he was dealing. He had a powerful sense that an attempt was being made to negate his prayer, to force his attention away from the girl, a pressure which lasted for a considerable period and left him exhausted. The experience alerted Gilbert to the possibility that Pauline was under some kind of psychic control and at their next meeting he challenged her with this. It turned out that she was terrified by his discovery for she had been warned that should she ever admit the truth about herself she would be made to suffer terribly.

The entire picture of Pauline's conditioning was only pieced together by Gilbert over many years. In addition to providing the appropriate medical and psychological support for her he had to begin to unravel a sophisticated and deep-seated control over her subconscious mind. These had even included a conditioning to sickness or suicide should anyone attempt to free her, to which was added a further attempt to control her involving the spirits of the dead. Although the Italian died in 1935, so extensive had been his 'programming' of her that his influence was not finally overcome until 1951. In fact she had been set up as a vital connection for the work of the society in England, almost like a telephone exchange through which various groups could make contact with one another by exploiting her psychic energies.

Careful to ensure his own medical and psychological well-being, Gilbert set himself to discover as much as he could about the work of this occult society. At one level he learned of the ways in which various groups made use of blackmail, usually for sexual reasons, to trap a person and exploit their psychic energies. It led him into a new understanding of the precise relationship between the psychic and the spiritual in man as well as of the relationship between our present sphere of existence and the realm of the dead. The more he learned, the more he was convinced that it was insufficient simply to account for his findings in psychological terms. Many of those involved had unquestionably been affected psychologically and Gilbert recognized that there was a clear correlation between immature or disturbed personalities and a susceptibility to the psychic control of others but he also knew that there was much more to it than this. His learning and understanding led him to see that as a Christian priest he was duty bound to attempt to arrest the influence of such a group and help those involved as best he could.

One level of response was to ensure protection for Pauline. She renewed her baptismal vows and was brought fully into the life of the Church and provided with a degree of physical protection. Gilbert knew she also needed psychic protection. To those unfamiliar with such language, to say nothing of the reality it attempts to describe, this will sound peculiar. Others, perhaps, with some awareness of their own psychic sense, will find it easier to grasp. It is therefore appropriate at this juncture to give some consideration to just what is understood by the realm of the psychic and how it relates to some of the unpleasantnesses he believed he was discovering through his ministry to this girl.

The psychic

> 'The psychic life of man has been far too long the happy hunting ground of the charlatan and the unscientific speculator . . .'

Thus Gilbert begins his account of the place of the psychic

in human life in one of the lectures he gave on the subject in the late 1940s. He believed that a first stage in understanding came from recognizing that the psychic is something quite natural within creation:

> '. . . and is concerned with relationship and communication between sensible units of life. We have become so accustomed to think in terms of communication only in those belonging to space which we have rationalised by visual observation, by weight and measure, that we rule out other possibilities, and limit our sensitiveness to the material and physical. The psychic is only the observation of immaterial reality that belongs to the created world of time-space . . . I only want to establish the fact that the psychic can be dealt with reasonably and rationally and can be discriminated and educated just as any other part of our make up and, if not rationally treated, will delude us and lead to the most startling errors.

He was quite clear that only such an account of the psychic could adequately account for the many experiences which had been thoroughly investigated and which could not simply be dismissed as 'psychological'. As far as he was concerned he was simply describing a non-material and quite natural reality, something which is experienced by many, whether Christian or not. Awareness of it varies from person to person but no one is free from its influence though he was quite clear that the more 'materialist' we have become the less aware we are likely to be.

As material reality is characterized by energy so there is also an energy associated with the psychic, otherwise it could not make itself known within the material. Such energies are perhaps experienced in the form of suggestions coming to the mind which some will clothe in forms supplied by the imagination, or may even be experienced in a physical way as in Macbeth: 'By the pricking of my thumbs I know some evil this way comes'. It is clear that some, occasionally referred to as 'sensitives', have a much stronger awareness of these energies than others. In itself that is of no significance, and of this Gilbert was quite adamant, for what matters is not the fact of what gifts we might have but how we use them. That highlights the essential difference between the spiritual and the psychic, for spirituality is about our total response to God, about how we use the whole of the natural order including the psychic.

Because the psychic is a natural realm of human activity it is not only Christians who have access to it nor could it possibly be claimed that only Christians try to use it well. Just as non-Christians are capable of using their physical gifts in the service of others so non-Christians with heightened psychic awareness can be among those who use such a gift to the benefit of their fellow humans. A clear example of this would be natural 'healers' who having recognized the close inter–reaction between the material and the immaterial seek to use psychic energy to effect physical and mental changes in the sick, often with surprising results. This is also the foundation of Christian healing whereby those called to exercise the ministry of healing recognize the psychic energies given by God and ask Him to use them to heal and make whole those for whom and with whom they pray. Most 'natural' healers are just as humble as the best Christian healers and know full well that the energies with which they co-operate are outside themselves, even though they have been given the gifts to discern and use them. The essential difference between the Christian healer and the natural healer is that the former would want to ascribe all the glory to God in Christ and then want to affirm that there is more to healing than simply the repair of bodies, though of course it is a start. Jesus himself commented that 'it is better for you to enter life maimed than with two hands to go to hell' (Mk.9.47). So psychic energies are part of the natural world and as with any other part can be used or abused.

Much of Gilbert's concern in the case of Pauline was with those, calling themselves magicians, who sought to abuse the natural psychic energies of creation. Magic is the attempt to harness psychic energy and to use it to take power. Gilbert's extensive study of the history of magic and the occult revealed how, over the centuries, there was built up worldwide a considerable body of teaching on the means of harnessing and controlling psychic energy for power. This knowledge formed a considerable body of teaching and he was at pains to stress that magic, as he encountered it, was a definite philosophy, not merely casual experimentation with unusual power. Rather it was a deliberate attempt not merely to harness but also to generate psychic energy. To this end it was necessary to have devotees and rites and all the paraphernalia of esoteric worship in which such groups appear to revel. The use of animal (and formerly human) sacrifice as an intrinsic part of magical rites or the build up of sexual frenzy are both part of the means of generating energy which others manipulate and use for their own power. Not all of those participating in such things realized their significance but those controlling them did and it was they whom Gilbert regarded as the greatest adversaries, not least because being himself psychically aware to an extreme degree he recognized an affinity with them:

> . . . remember that those who might by their natural gifts and vocation become the greatest contemplatives might, if they go wrong, become the greatest forces of evil. Hence the great danger of those who have a natural religious attrait playing about with the uncanny, because their very capacity for God can so easily be turned by the devil into his service.

As time went on in his dealings with Pauline and especially in his experience of actual opposition to his prayer he gradually realized that he was not merely dealing with magicians who were manipulating and abusing natural forces for their own ends, but that this was an actual encounter with evil: men and women, albeit few in number, who rode upon the backs of the larger circle of magicians and extended the nature and range of their activities often in sinister ways. This growing realization took Gilbert in his reading back to the experience of the Biblical and Patristic traditions regarding such things, notably the experience of the Desert Fathers.

This new awareness was not just of sinful, i.e. fallen, nature at work but that which is actually rebellious, organizing in the name of the enemy of God and seeking to use such powers as they could take for themselves against God and the Church. They were much more advanced than were the magicians whom previously he had encountered. For a start they were involved in much more than just psychic manipulation, being also active in the area of spiritualism whereby they sought to make use of the psychic energies of the dead as part of their means to power and control of the living. It was their belief that even this energy could be harnessed to which end many of their rites included animal sacrifice or involved the use of mediums. Among Gilbert's writings from this period is a forty-two page paper on the cognizance of disembodied souls in which he sets out as logically as possible the theory which underlies the practice of certain groups employing the energies of the dead. He gives instances of the practice at the present time as well as offering a brief survey of its history and how well known it is in certain magic and other esoteric writings. In the end he emphasizes that his own experience is the only authority he could offer as surety for such things. Others with related experience have suggested that in such matters his experience is a reliable guide but it is one of those areas which seems to be closed to investigation.

Among his other writings are notes which show that he accepted the existence of various psychic channels initiated and controlled by different magic groups in Britain and elsewhere. Various centres could be identified with the irruption of these energies, some of them traditional sites of heathen magic. Gilbert sought to 'tune in' to this psychic waveband in order to break up or block the energies. There is a clear analogy here with the way in which various governments seek to 'jam' radio broadcasts by interfering with wavelengths. Throughout the rest of his life Gilbert tried to do this, and the experience derived from this clearly had an effect upon his health. People were often told he was 'under the weather' when he was feeling the pressure he encountered in this particular form of the conflict. He was seeking to turn back the energies upon those who had originated them, never by seeking to match magic with magic but by drawing strength from prayer and the sacramental life of the Church, not just his own prayer but also that of intercessors who supported him with their prayer though never participating in the actual work. The only one who ever shared in the work directly was Mother Mary Clare. Gilbert believed that, in some clear and positive way, prayer broke up malevolent psychic energy and also introduced light where hitherto there had been only darkness. It was more than just a neutralizing of evil. In this way the presence of contemplatives served to bring evil to the light, revealing it for what it is.

Spiritual conflict

To most people a description of such things seems fantastic, though some may recall the works of C.S. Lewis or the novels of Charles Williams. In fact Gilbert was critical of Williams' writings on these matters, believing that he over-personalized the nature of the conflict and did not sufficiently emphasize the ultimate power of overcoming which is directly derived from the cross and resurrection of Jesus.

Throughout his extensive writings on such matters Gilbert makes it clear that in most of his work at this psychic level he was contending against human agencies. Gilbert was well aware that the desert tradition of encounter with evil and the spiritual conflict emphasized the danger of delusion; he also knew enough to recognize that many of those involved in these things were simply looking for excitement of one kind or another and had no real interest in the magic *per se*. Others too were themselves so deluded that they couldn't separate reality and fantasy. There were some, though, who had to be taken seriously and not least in their relation to the devil. He unquestionably accepted the existence of the devil as an actual personification of evil force, related to which were demons, which, like their master, were fallen angels. His understanding of this was fully set out in a major paper prepared for a conference of the Fellowship of St Alban and St Sergius and published in a collection called 'The Angels of Light and the Powers of Darkness' in 1952. The book was edited by Eric Mascall and other contributors included Prof. Hodges and the Russian orthodox priest, later archbishop, Basil Krivoshein. Gilbert's contribution '*Angels and Demons in Human Life*', although seemingly concerned with presenting his angelological and demonological theory, reveals a developing understanding of how all his experience of darkness and unpleasantness could be made to make sense within the boundaries of a theology and would repay careful study. Of one thing he was absolutely certain and that is the final overcoming by Christ of all evil. For this reason he believed that it was important not to focus attention upon the spiritual enemy but instead to concentrate on the power of Christ's death and resurrection.

From his earliest days in Poplar other peculiar happenings were referred to him, such as apparent hauntings and cases of possession. Almost invariably Gilbert was satisfied after examination that some alternative explanation could adequately account for the manifestations. He believed scepticism to be the only proper way to approach such work, an attitude he strongly commended to all who were drawn into this form of ministry. His experience at Eynsham and his knowledge of the work of the Satanist Society had taught him not to go looking for trouble. As the workload grew he adopted a policy of accepting requests for help only from bishops, and when he was engaged in an investigation or an exorcism, he always ensured that the diocesan was kept fully in the picture. He also made it a rule never to engage in this form of ministry without the active participation of a Christian doctor.

One of the limiting features of his early work was the absence within the Church of England of practical experience of these ministries and an equal absence of theory. The only forms for exorcism available to him were Roman Catholic. He therefore set about the task of translating and revising these and it is his work which underlies all the liturgical forms relating to the ministries of deliverance used within the Church today.

A lot of nonsense has been written about exorcism, and harmful things have been undertaken by the unwise in the period since Gilbert's active ministry, not least by some in the Charismatic movement. In most cases the reason for things going wrong lies between an over-active imagination, what has been called a 'devils under the bed' syndrome which sees things which are just not there or which has no actual ability of discernment, and an undue and inappropriate emphasis upon the power of those praying rather than on the redemptive power of the risen Christ. Of all the books produced on this subject since his death none would have delighted him more than *Renewal and the Powers of Darkness* by Cardinal Suenens, which also seeks to set the theory and practice of this ministry within the proper context of the paschal faith of the Church and an appropriate angelology.

By the time he was working at St Anne's he was not only being consulted by bishops, but also by the government. Intelligence reports had indicated that Hitler and other members of the Third Reich were making use of occult practices. Gilbert was consulted to discover just what all this might mean. It is an adequate testimony both to the measure of seriousness with which Gilbert's efforts to present his work as clearly as possible had been viewed and also to the fact that there was no one else at that time experienced enough to take the work on. He did make efforts to share some of it with others. At St Anne's he was reunited with Max Petitpierre and brought him into a full sharing of the work, a ministry he continued to exercise in his own right for the rest of his life. In 1947 Max became a monk of the Anglican Benedictine monastery at Nashdom, taking the name of Dom Robert, and Gilbert attempted to recruit one or two priests to replace him as a partner. This was to prove far from easy and he was to know more than one disappointment. In part this was caused by the tendency for priests to become unhealthily interested in what they imagined to be the sensational nature of the work. Gilbert did not believe that there was anything sensational about the work; it was simply a matter of the ordinary healing ministry of the Church applying the victory of Christ in every area of human and sub-human activity. Of course any encounter with the demonic or the disturbed required care, for which reason Gilbert believed it should only be engaged in by experienced and mature priests. The first requirement for the work was an absolute faith in the final overcoming of evil by Christ allied to an appropriate asceticism of body, psyche and spirit. The second was an almost total disinterest in the subject; only in this way could priests be well protected against the prince of lies. Increasingly he believed the work should be wholly under episcopal control. Some of the disturbing excesses in recent years in this area of ministry, and especially amongst charismatic groups where spiritual excitement triumphs over spiritual discipline, could have been avoided had even these basic requirements been met.

As a pioneer in this field Gilbert was often asked to give lectures to groups of clergy and throughout the late 1940s he travelled widely doing so. His talks were often received with scepticism however. The prevailing philosophical climate and the manifest tendency of theology to limp along behind it, both of which were being increasingly dominated by logical positivism and a repudiation of metaphysics, tended towards an *a priori* rejection of Gilbert and his concerns. To this was allied a feeling that he was just an old eccentric who could safely be dismissed, preference being given to the new psychology which was for the first time becoming available in popular form.

Conflict with the Church

Some of the difficulties faced by Gilbert emerged when he and Max were invited to give evidence in 1954 to a sub-committee on demonology of a Church Commission on Healing. In the first place he must take some blame for his contribution to the work of the commission's being limited to the consideration of demonology. Some of his other pioneering work on healing quite unrelated to demons might have been most useful in bringing life to what was eventually to be a singularly dull and uninspiring report. However he had earned a reputation for himself as being only concerned with evil and his only contribution was thus severely limited.

They produced a clear and comprehensive account of their experience in relation to the whole question of evil and the demonic, setting out how theory and practice cohered, relating it both to orthodox theology and the whole history of the Christian tradition in regard to such things. They must have realized from the beginning, however, that their views would not gain much of a hearing in the light of the man appointed to examine their material. Professor Ian Ramsey was the most explicitly committed anti-metaphysician among contemporary Christian academics. A pioneer among Christians seeking to do justice to logical positivism and the question of religious language, his objections to their accounts were in the main concerned with the relationship of the psychological to the psychic and the whole problem of how experience is to be evaluated. He felt that too much reliability had to be placed upon unverifiable experience-claims. The 'principle of verification' still reigned supreme in 1954 and as a committed empiricist it would have been highly unlikely had Ramsey overridden his dependency upon it in considering the material presented to him. Accordingly all nine of his objections to their accounts derive from this and it served to highlight a significant credibility gap between those who were attempting to give a reasoned account of experience and those who quite without experience were employing non-Christian principles and theory to dismiss *a priori* a significant aspect of the Christian tradition. As late as 1963 Gilbert observed that the current intellectual climate which the Bishops seemed to have swallowed wholesale meant that there was hardly one of their number who took the reality of evil at all seriously. It is perhaps ironical and not without importance that the whole logical positivist school with its verification principle collapsed so thoroughly a generation later. In passing it is worth noting that in 1975 an Open Letter on Exorcism was addressed to the bishops and General Synod of the Church of England. Written by two Cambridge theologians Geoffrey Lampe and Don Cupitt it sought to have exorcism officially outlawed as wholly incompatible with the world-view of twentieth century Europe. Although the writers were no doubt correct in expressing concern about the irresponsible use of such a ministry, it was once again a case of theory sitting in judgement upon experience. Although both writers were sincere and attractive people it is certain that someone such as Gilbert would have seen significance in the fact that within a year one of them would have cast doubts upon the Trinity as the foundation of the Christian faith and the other eventually announce that he no longer believed in God in any objective sense. Experience, theology and spirituality hang close together.

Less fashionable philosophers, though no less eminent than their empiricist colleagues, such as Prof. Bert Hodges and Prof. H.D. Lewis, were able to be of enormous help to Gilbert by continuing to provide a philosophical framework into which Gilbert's experience and theory could fit. Lewis in particular has been long used to treading a lone furrow in his concern for the concept of the soul and its survival of death and Hodges had contributed his own paper to the conference and book on angels and demons.

The report of the Church's Commission on Divine Healing was published in 1958. As continues to happen to this day, it was the, albeit muted, references to the ministry of deliverance which attracted most of the media attention, a clear example of the lure of the prince of this world. Gilbert appeared on the BBC television programme 'Panorama' and was made the subject of a full-page feature in the *Sunday Dispatch*. The report was welcomed by the Guild of St Raphael, a group which has been concerned with the ministry of healing for many years, and for whom Gilbert wrote some helpful articles on exorcism during the 1950s. Its episcopal head was the Bishop of Wakefield, John Ramsbotham, one of the few bishops with whom Gilbert was able to feel at ease in speaking of his work. It was for Bishop John that he wrote a long memorandum on exorcism which was, without due attribution, subsequently used as the basis of the *Exeter Report* on exorcism in 1973. Equally, the forms for exorcism contained in that report are those originally prepared by Gilbert, though Max Petitpierre as editor of the report omitted to acknowledge this.

By the early 1950s Gilbert recognized that he had little support from within the Church and the frustrations engendered by this recognition exacerbated the strains already upon him by virtue of the work itself. There seemed to be a new wave of activity associated with various magic groups and this was to preoccupy him for the following five years. He was now in his late sixties and, although his ascetic lifestyle helped him spiritually, it cannot have been wholly good for his body. Increased physical weakness was made worse by the pressure of broken relationships notably between him and Max Petitpierre. Gilbert believed that Max was seeking to sensationalize the work, speaking too much about ghosts and taking insufficient account of the reality of evil in relation to magic and although Max wrote *The Times* obituary of Gilbert and spoke of him most warmly, Gilbert forbade his fellow workers to have any contact with him.

Another fellow worker who was to cause enormous distress was a nun with whom he worked for a short time in 1954, a member of one of the communities to whom he acted as a confessor. She had a training and psychic awareness which suggested her to be an ideal partner, but in seeking to involve her Gilbert made a serious error of judgement which was to bring home to him yet more powerfully the need for great caution in choosing men and women for this work. Emotional immaturity is very quickly revealed by it and great harm can be done by those with good intentions. In this instance the nun left her community, and although she was not dispensed from her vows, circumstances were such that Gilbert officiated at her subsequent marriage, an action which led Fr O'Brien SSJE to petition the Archbishop of Canterbury for his excommunication. Dr Fisher received from Gilbert a full account of the precise circumstances and responded in his favour though, in order to maintain discretion, did not inform O'Brien of the full circumstances, which unfortunately served to ensure further years of misunderstanding between him and Gilbert. A further twist to this tale came a couple of years later when one of those involved made an attempt to destroy Gilbert's records of the case, an attempt that was fortunately only partially successful. Such events of course were deeply wounding to him.

In his last years Gilbert was too old and infirm to be directly involved in active work, whether investigating claims or taking part in exorcisms. In fact he performed relatively few actual exorcisms as such; usually other facets of the ministry of healing were more appropriate, the number of cases of possession being extremely small. That in itself needs constantly to be borne in mind, not least by certain charismatic groups who often attribute every manifestation of peculiarity to possession, whereas Gilbert would assert that in almost every case the reason would be either psychological or as the result of some psychic disturbance or other. It is an area where illusion and delusion abound. Emotional maturity needs to be allied to the appropriate asceticism and experience spoken of above. Without these things, illusion can have and has had serious consequences.

Although himself no longer active in such things he did attempt to offer such help as he could to those who were. More than one person was prepared by him for some aspect or other of the ministry of deliverance and it is a tribute to his knowledge and wisdom that matters invariably went exactly as he indicated. Others who had experienced peculiar psychic manifestations or who had known unusual spiritual pressure, sometimes even in the form of demonic assault were also able to consult him and receive an understanding of their experience which enabled them to set it within the context of their life and prayer. At every stage the intent of his ministry was pastoral, to bring people liberation and restore them to wholesomeness. Those who knew no better were happy to dismiss him as a crank, as no doubt they would dismiss the realities with which he was dealing, but his writings do not allow so superficial a judgement and dismissal. Together with other writings on healing (a ministry he was exercising long before it assumed its present importance) they are an important legacy to the Church in her continuing work of proclaiming the Kingdom in word and deed.

A valid criticism of his work might be that at certain times he became too involved, falling foul of his own warnings. In an effort to communicate something to others, at a time when he was feeling isolated, he undoubtedly tended to talk too much about the more sensational aspects of the work and these lapses probably account for such reputation as he had. His 'case-histories', too, suggest that he was not always as detached as he knew he ought to be and that in particular there were times when he did not control an over-active imagination as he ought. Certainly there was one occasion when he was rebuked by Max on this account and Gilbert was forced to concede the point, though more than anything else it highlighted the fact that Gilbert operated alone so much of the time and in an area of activity in which more than most he needed help and guidance.

Orthodox allies

In the earliest days the necessary theological support had been provided by Fr William. In particular he had introduced Gilbert to the writings of the desert fathers and the monastic tradition in which the spiritual conflict was fully recognized. The whole contemplative and monastic tradition was itself deeply rooted within the Patristic writings for only right belief could enable the Church to recognize evil – a lesson from the 4th century that remains permanently true. After Fr William's death, Gilbert experienced a profound sense of theological isolation and it was only at the end of the 1940s, when he began to make closer contact with Christians of the

Eastern churches that he began to encounter those who spoke the same language as himself about the nature of the spiritual conflict and the reality of evil.

This came about through membership of the Fellowship of St Alban and St Sergius, at whose conferences he often spoke and where he met Fr Georges Florovsky and Vladimir Lossky, notable Russian theologians based in Paris. There also grew up a most important friendship with the young Russian priest who came to England in 1949 as chaplain to the Fellowship, Fr Anthony Bloom, later Archbishop and Metropolitan of Sourozh. Their first meeting took place one evening in the clergy house at Southwark, and so caught up were they in conversation together that there was no public transport still running to take Fr Anthony home. Both men discovered the other to be one whom they could respect and from whom they had much to learn. Fr Anthony still speaks of him in exalted terms tinged with slight awe, not least perhaps by virtue of one experience of Gilbert which continues to amuse and astonish him even after more than twenty years. It happened at a time when Fr Anthony was generally unwell and on the occasion of a visit by Gilbert he happened to mention that he had some back trouble. Gilbert replied with the suggestion that he might do something about it. He asked Fr Anthony to stand up and turn away; Gilbert took him by the shoulders and then putting his mouth against the part of the back causing the trouble, blew powerfully. It was as if he was attempting to inflate the bishop with new energy. The amazing thing was that it worked, something which Fr Anthony, formerly a medical doctor, received joyfully, even if without comprehension.

Fr Anthony found Gilbert's experience of the conflict with the realities of evil something which tied up with his own Orthodox tradition and he very much appreciated the fact that although Gilbert was wholly in earnest in his conversation about evil, possession and the devil, he was also clearly able to laugh at himself.

However important, the contacts with the Orthodox played a relatively small part in Gilbert's life during the 1950s. In the main it was a time of heightened isolation, in which friends avoided him or let him down. He knew full well what those in authority thought of him and to this was added a real spiritual depression, in which for a time at least he felt increasingly cut off from God. It was in this sense a real night of faith for him and one which he began to feel must end in failure. It seems likely that with his seventieth birthday in the offing he was beginning to plan for retirement and the end of active ministry, something which seemed even more inevitable with the breakdown of his health in early 1957. Although he still believed he had important work to do it must have seemed at the time that retirement was inevitable and that his life and work would end with disappointment and, in some ways, failure. 1957 was very much a year of depression and desolation; it was very much a broken reed who, one afternoon in November, stopped by Waterloo Station at the suggestion of a friend to meet a nun, Mother Mary Clare.

6

Along the Road of Solitude
1958–63

The Carmelite Inheritance

Gilbert was changed by his experience of the darkness of the years from 1945. Gone forever was that severity bordering upon arrogance which had so repelled a decade earlier, although by most normal standards he remained a somewhat formidable figure. If he was tempered in some aspects of his being it is also true that in others he had been fashioned anew and that spiritually at least, it had been a definite means to growth. To one rooted in the Carmelite tradition this must have come as no surprise although the nature of nights of faith is that such only becomes apparent afterwards. St John of the Cross describing the passive night of the Spirit wrote:

> Darkness has deprived it of all things – yet love and faith, now burning within it, drawing the heart towards the Beloved, influence and guide it, and make it fly upwards to God along the road of solitude, while it knows neither how nor by what means that is done. (*Dark Night of the Soul*)

Gilbert's great love of the writings of St John of the Cross stemmed above all from his experience of the realities which they describe so clearly. He was a great expositor of the Carmelite tradition and in the remaining years of his life they were to be the foundation of all that he was enabled to do with the Sisters of the Love of God. He was careful however to stress that the writings of the saint need to be approached with some caution. He did not feel that people should be introduced to St John or St Teresa until they had at least spent some time in regular and disciplined prayer and that there was always a danger that some people would imagine themselves further advanced than they actually were by reading those works which belong more appropriately to others. For this reason he drew up a helpful suggested order of reading of the works of St Teresa and St John:

1) *Dark Night of the Soul*, Book 1, Chapters 1–10.
2) *Ascent of Mount Carmel*, Book 1.
3) *Dark Night of the Soul*, Book 1, Chapters 11–14.
4) *Spiritual Sentences and Maxims*.
5) *Letters and Poems*.
6) St Teresa, *Way of Perfection*.
7) St Teresa, *Interior Castle*, Mansions I–V.
8) *Living Flame of Love*, Books I–III.
9) *Spiritual Canticle*, earlier stanzas.
10) *Ascent of Mount Carmel*, Books 2 and 3.
    Dark Night, Book 2.
    St Teresa, Mansions VI and VII.

In addition to his evident familiarity with the Carmelites he also had extensive knowledge of and drew heavily upon the works of the Flemish mystic Jan van Ruysbroek and St Catherine of Siena. These four major representatives of the western tradition of spirituality were to play a prominent part in the teaching he was soon to be called to give at Fairacres.

The meeting with Mother Mary Clare marked the end of his long period of solitary night. After their initial meeting they maintained their relationship by courtesy of the postal and telecommunication services and in the following two years many hundreds of letters passed between them. Their letters reveal that at first their relationship was very much a father-daughter one, though in the course of time and through sharing so much it became more like that of brother and sister.

At this time SLG was still being guided by a warden from the SSJE community, and because Gilbert was very much *persona non grata* as far as their Superior was concerned it was only by a slow process that Gilbert could be drawn into the orbit of their life, though it is clear that from the beginning this was what Mary Clare wanted. The initial contacts were made at the convent at Burwash where he went for a number of retreats, the first being in 1958.

Mary Clare had known psychic experiences akin to those of Gilbert and she found it most helpful to have someone who could help her to make sense of them. She also referred to him a number of sisters who had run into spiritual problems. He already had some experience of ministering to women's communities, and in addition to his work with the Community of the Holy Name at Malvern, he had more recently become confessor extraordinary to the Buxted house of the Community of St Mary the Virgin, whose mother-house was at Wantage. From the beginning of their relationship it was clear to him that SLG were different from these other communities, with their particular Carmelite inheritance, carefully led for so long by Fr Cary. Gilbert set about a careful study of the teachings of the former warden and in his later work with the community was always at pains to emphasize the note of continuity between his illustrious predecessor and himself.

The new link with SLG seemed to rejuvenate Gilbert almost at once and he laid aside any plans he might have been forming about retirement. In 1949 Gilbert had decided that he wanted to sell the house at Wallingford, and he had moved Sylvia instead to Buxted in Sussex. She was most unhappy about the move and it is clear that at this time their relationship was at its worst. It meant that at 58 and largely alone, she had to build a new life for herself. Many of their friends were upset and cross with Gilbert for the astonishing insensitivity he manifested towards her though, as it turned out, she was able to settle quite well in Sussex and Gilbert was able to get home slightly more often.

He became a familiar figure to passengers on the Buxted-London line, although by all accounts villagers often tended to shy away from him on the platform for fear that with his loud and penetrating voice he would ask them an embarrassing question. Buxted was proving a fortuitous home base being close to Burwash though he always needed transporting wherever he went, his earliest attempts at driving having resulted in the family placing a ban upon him sitting anywhere other than in a passenger seat. He also enjoyed family gatherings at Buxted and one particular occasion is recalled in which after tea together he insisted that they all join him in his little oratory for a short service, in the course of which he actually preached them a homily. There cannot be many who would have dared to attempt such a thing, nor families willing to endure it.

Two monasteries

Another opportunity provided by the situation of Buxted was its close proximity to Crawley Down, home of the nascent community at whose inception he had been present in 1938. Progress here had been slow. The superior, Fr Robert Gofton-Salmond had first come into contact with Gilbert as a parish priest in the East End where Gilbert had done an exorcism for him. In 1937 he had helped him find a location for his monastery. From the beginning Fr Robert seemed to have no clear direction in mind for the new community and was surprised at his profession in 1953 to hear the preacher, Fr Geoffrey Curtis C.R. describe it as a contemplative foundation. He accepted the description but without enthusiasm, though he knew that Gilbert shared the hope for it as such. During the period after 1945 Gilbert had paid a number of visits to Crawley Down and his friendship with Fr Robert was an important means of support during those years.

Mention has also been made of the importance he attached to his friendship with Fr Anthony Bloom and his growing awareness of the Orthodox tradition. One of the most significant developments in his appreciation of this tradition came to him through a book which appeared in 1958, *The Undistorted Image*, a translation of a French life of the great Athonite hermit and teacher, the Staretz Silouan. The author, the Archimandrite Sophrony had once been a disciple of the Staretz and now lived in Paris. Gilbert at once recognized the value of the book, both in terms of the greatness of Silouan but also in what it revealed about the author. He was clearly a man of prayer and perception who knew something of the reality of the spiritual conflict. Thus Gilbert was delighted to hear in 1959 that Fr Sophrony was coming to live in Essex, founding an Orthodox monastery at Tolleshunt Knights, and as soon as he arrived he went to visit him.

Fr Sophrony was born in Russia in 1896 and, growing up amidst the crisis of the Revolution, was trained as a painter at the Moscow School of Fine Arts. In 1921 he emigrated to France where he exhibited with moderate success before throwing his art on one side in a spiritual search which led him to the holy Greek peninsula of Mt Athos and the Orthodox monasteries there in which he encountered and was a disciple of the Staretz Silouan. Here he remained for 22 years, the last 7 of which were spent as a hermit. Ill health forced him back to Paris before he was able to come to England as a pioneer of Orthodox monasticism in this country. He is a man of rare spiritual qualities, one who has been widely recognized as a great teacher of prayer within the Orthodox tradition but whose influence has extended beyond its boundaries and brought to him people such as Thomas Merton. He belongs however to what might be called the 'hard line' school of Orthodoxy with regard to ecumenism. A visitor from a different tradition may indeed receive the help he is seeking but for his pains might also expect a polemic on the evil of the *Filioque* and those traditions employing it. Yet from the earliest days of their relationship Fr Sophrony recognized Gilbert's priesthood, even to the extent of inviting him into the sanctuary of the monastery church to give the blessing, a privilege subsequently granted to no other non-Orthodox. Although now very frail in his old age Fr Sophrony continues to speak of Gilbert in the highest terms, something echoed by the Orthodox lay woman Lady Namier, or Iulia de Beausobre as she was formerly known. Herself a remarkable lady, she did not find Anglicans or the western tradition in general something she fully understood or felt that Orthodox could learn much from until she met Gilbert and later read his book *The Face of Love*. A note in her biography refers to the great impression Gilbert made upon her and in a most positive review of his book she commented that for the first time she had encountered a western book from which the Orthodox might benefit. The respect was reciprocated, for Gilbert greatly enjoyed her book *Flame in the Snow*, a life of the great Russian Saint Seraphim of Sarov.

Indebted though he was to the insights and friendship of men such as Fr Anthony or Fr Sophrony, he nevertheless remained rooted within his own western tradition and was ever wary of recommending too much Orthodox theology to those who consulted him. To a great extent this was because he recognized romanticism to be a special danger in dealing with the Orthodox, the aesthetic and mysterious appeal of the liturgy being so great. It would, he thought, be far better for people to discover the riches of their own traditions before exploring those of others, and in speaking at Fellowship conferences he urged people against spiritual syncretism. On the other hand he also urged that western Christians recognize that for the first millenium of the Christian era the Church had been one and that there was much which was common to the whole Church which many in the west knew little or nothing of, and which could only serve to enrich their churches.

Reading and writing

Although many people only ever knew Gilbert as a somewhat austere and formidable priest, he could also be good company and to many, a much valued friend. He may have lived somewhat frugally but he knew a good wine and enjoyed taking friends to the Athenaeum. One of the characteristics which most appealed to his friends was an ability in practical matters 'Nobody except Gilbert could ever get the boiler to work properly' is a saying which well illustrates this facet of the man and it goes well with his love of photography and landscape gardening. He also continued to read widely, especially in history and philosophy and kept an eye on developments in theology. He was among the first to recognize the significance of Dietrich Bonhoeffer, the first edition of whose influential *Letters and Papers from Prison* he read in 1953. Gilbert saw Bonhoeffer as belonging to the true succession of martyrs of the Church and he made extensive use in his teaching of Bonhoeffer's important concept of, what he preferred to call, 'unpietistic' Christianity, a translation he believed was more accurate than the more familiar 'religionless', popularized a decade later by Bishop John Robinson. This preference has been more than substantiated by the appearance in English of Eberhard Bethge's definitive biography of Bonhoeffer.

In addition to theology he also read a good deal of modern literature and many of his addresses in this period contain illustrations from the works of Eliot or from sources as diverse as *Waiting for Godot*, *The Uses of Literacy*, the writings of R.G. Collingwood and *Winnie the Pooh*. He even attempted to write some poetry, or at least something that is akin to a combination of poetry and meditation. Some of it is moderately successful though he would never have pretended that it was better than it is. In fact they are little more than exercises in affective prayer with additional attention given to form, but he enjoyed their production and some of them are still published under the apt title *Rythmic Prayers*.

In 1957 he was approached by Mowbrays with a view to his writing their Lent book for 1959. This was to be *The Face of Love*, a series of extended meditations of an affective kind based upon the traditional devotion of the Stations of the Cross. He was seeking to make it a collection more akin to the illuminative stage of prayer than the earlier *Pilgrims Book of Prayers*, though the development is not always quite so clear. He was satisfied with the book although expressed a hope at some stage it might be tidied up a little, a work eventually undertaken after his death by Mother Mary Clare.

He very much hoped that Mowbrays would be willing to publish a sequel appropriate to the unitive stage of prayer and was somewhat disappointed when they rejected the idea, even though sales of the Lent book had been good. As it was, Gilbert was never to complete the final part of the anticipated trilogy although he drew up various plans for it, nor was he able to produce a book for lay people intended as an introduction to the principles of prayer in its different stages or phases, although after his death such a work, unfortunately not yet published, was compiled. As it was the early 1960s may well have proved an inappropriate time for such works, the theological climate being dominated as it was by the after-effects of *Soundings* and *Honest to God*.

In addition to writings on healing and deliverance he produced a number of papers on prayer and related themes throughout the 1950s, including a chapter on prayer in a symposium on the work of a hospital chaplain, whilst still maintaining his extensive personal ministry based on St Alphege. In early 1959 the incumbent, Fr Gain, became ill with brain tumours which led to his death in June of that year and Gilbert acted as priest-in-charge of the parish up to the time of the institution of the new vicar Fr Eric Mathieson. Not surprisingly the new priest elected to have his vicarage restored to something more akin to normality and Gilbert moved into the small flat adjacent to the parish hall. Although it still served as a useful *pied-a-terre*, the relationship between Gilbert and the parish was inevitably changed by these new circumstances.

Southwark diocese received a new bishop in 1959, and Gilbert was dismayed to discover that Dr Mervyn Stockwood was in the habit of visiting what he called a 'Christian spiritualist' in order to make contact with his departed mother. He also took exception to the setting up of a body within the Church for exploration into psychical and spiritualist research and wrote to the Church of England's pre-eminent canon lawyer, the Worshipful E. Garth Moore, to see what could be done to stop it. In fact Chancellor Moore was soon to become President of the new body and was unable to sympathize with Gilbert's anxieties. It is hard to believe that Gilbert would not have been pleased with some of the subsequent work of the Churches Fellowship for Psychic and Spiritual Studies, a body which has helped a good number of people make sense of their own experiences, enabling them to remain within the mainstream churches rather than becoming involved with spiritualist groups.

Mystical theology

Lent 1962 was the occasion of Gilbert's first official work at Fairacres, a course of addresses on the spiritual tradition.

He recognized this as a moment of significance in a letter to Mother Mary Clare:

> It is all very miraculous for me to look back. I have always felt that in some way my vocation was to be used in preparing the way for revival and now in the partnership and strength of your co-operation it does seem to be coming into reality – we must go on in patience and joy.

He was clearly beginning to perceive the community to be the place where his concerns could find an adequate expression and reception, thus ensuring the continuity of the work which he believed had begun with Fr William, something which brought him great joy. The community also helped him survive a serious illness in later 1961 and during his convalescence at Burwash he wrote to Mother Mary Clare: 'If God is giving me time, I feel I have much to say'. No one who heard him in the following years could doubt that.

In his work with the sisters he aimed at bringing them a deeper understanding and participation in what he called 'the one great tradition' of the spiritual life. He derived the phrase from Dom Cuthbert Butler's *Western Mysticism* and it referred to that collection of spiritual maxims and teachings which had come to the fore in the life of the Church. However the one tradition was not merely a collection of names and books, it was also the means to participation in the life of prayer. The writings of the saints are not there for examination and analysis so much as to invite the readers to follow, a summons to live the gospel. It was this understanding, added to the experience of living under the aegis of the CR Rule in South Africa which enabled Gilbert from the earliest days to place so strong an emphasis upon the need for an ordered life of prayer.

Gilbert's own experience of the one great tradition had been through the Carmelites and other western writers including those of the English school. In the light of his encounters with the Orthodox during the 1950s he made increasing use of the eastern tradition, though in recommending it to others he was at pains to stress that only when we are wholly familiar with our own tradition should we begin to learn something of that of others. He would surely have been anxious about the dangers of people becoming fascinated by the current proliferation of Orthodox literature when so much of the western tradition in all its riches remains unknown; he knew only too well the romantic fascination of the Orthodox.

On the other hand there is also a proper recognition to be made of the fact that up to the division of Christendom in 1054 the Church was one, and much from the period prior to this split is common to the whole Church, even if some of it has largely lain dormant in the west. Thus for Gilbert the way into the eastern experience was by first entering the western tradition and discovering the common Biblical and Patristic roots and using this as a foundation from which to advance into the other tradition.

In coming to a deeper appreciation of this way of understanding the roots of spirituality Gilbert knew that he owed most to Fr William of Glasshampton rather than to the mainstream of spiritual life within the catholic movement of the Church of England. Gilbert had already realized by the time of his ordination that this movement had substantially changed from its own roots in the Oxford movement of the mid-19th century. At the popular level the theological concern of its tractarian fathers had largely given way to an unquestioning copying of Roman scholastic theology and liturgical practices, many of which were the incidentals of catholic faith. A concern to discover the roots of Anglican life in the writings of the Fathers, something to the fore in the early days of the movement with its rediscovery of the significance of the Caroline divines, had in many instances become little more than a series of attempts to ape Roman practices, many of which were in any case younger than Anglicanism itself.

The prevailing spiritual climate within the catholic movement was largely determined by the available Roman models and these were substantially post-Tridentine imports. Generations of anglo-catholics grew up with prayer books setting out stylized 'methods' of meditation to match equally stylized post-Tridentine extra-liturgical forms of devotional exercise. Though such patterns no doubt proved helpful to some, they represented only a small part of the entire Christian spiritual heritage and clearly many souls found them restrictive and inappropriate to their needs.

As Fr William grew in his vocation and made the move from being a friar through to being a solitary, so his experience of prayer also changed. What was appropriate to an active vocation clearly no longer satisfied, and he began a study of early monasticism. Convinced of the need for an enclosed contemplative community for men he explored the tradition of contemplative life from the earliest days of the settlements in the deserts of Egypt through to the origins of the Benedictine life in the fifth century, greatly enlarging his understanding of the patterns of contemplative life in the tradition of the whole church, east and west.

During his regular visits to Glasshampton Gilbert was able to enter into an appreciation of these things and in turn they proved formative in his own grasp of the place and importance of contemplatives in the life of the Church. He maintained that this influence had been the most significant of all in his work, especially his contact with the works of Cassian and the Cappadocian fathers. Thus he was brought into a familiarity with Patristic writings at a time when they were predominantly the preserve of academics. To him their significance lay in their being of practical value. He claimed that it was only by being rooted in the Patristic writings that he was able to hold a true course through the multiplicity of techniques and controversies of the 19th century writings which were so much the spiritual vogue in the early part of the century.

He was especially delighted by the publication of Fr Louis Bouyer's volume on the history of the spirituality of the New Testament and the Fathers, believing that it embodied precisely the concerns and understanding which had come to be his own throughout the course of his ministry. In practical terms this influence was eventually to have a significant effect upon the subsequent development of SLG, complementing the Carmelite tradition in which they already stood, and upon the refounding of CSWG.

The One Great Tradition

His rootedness in the writings and history of monasticism from the Patristic period meant yet another aspect in common with the Orthodox. With them he also came to a yet deeper understanding of the concept of tradition. He already saw it as being formed of the two elements of the writings of the saints and the pattern of training required for the life of prayer, to which was now added a third, that of tradition as a participation in the continuing work of the Holy Spirit in the life of the Church. Fr Georges Florovsky, whom Gilbert knew from the Fellowship of St Alban and St Sergius expressed this understanding thus:

> Ultimately, tradition is a continuity of the abiding presence of the Holy Spirit in the Church, a continuity of guidance and illumination. . . . This same spirit, the Spirit of Truth which 'spake by the prophets', which guided the apostles, is still guiding the Church . . .

For Gilbert this meant that there is a contemporaneity about the scriptures and writings of the saints which makes their experience accessible to ourselves. The Holy Spirit who guided them is still present to us as much as to them; each epiclesis in the Eucharist is a new participation in the realities of the day of Pentecost. To read the scriptures or the works of the saints is to discover that in the power of the Holy Spirit they can speak directly to our condition, even though the circumstances of our living are very different indeed from those in which they were written. Echoing an Orthodox understanding, Gilbert maintained that in the absence of a spiritual father, the writings of the saints could safely be used to guide our prayer, for they are those who speak 'out of knowledge'. Tradition is a participation in a living community in which the departed are just as much our friends as the living. In so far as we make ourselves ready to receive the gift of contemplative prayer we shall be enabled by the power of the Holy Spirit to know for ourselves the realities of which the scriptures and the saints have spoken. Thus tradition is seen as a participation in something essentially dynamic and at every stage of his teaching ministry the dominant thrust was an overwhelming awareness of the reality of the sanctifying work of the Holy Spirit in the present life and experience of the Church.

To almost all the sisters such an understanding of tradition, which Gilbert offered them in his initial encounters, was something quite new and for Gilbert too it was the first time in which he was giving expression to something which had been gradually growing within him; in his mid seventies he was discovering new things and a fluency which had previously been absent. He couldn't deny that it all seemed to belong to a definite pattern in which there appeared at last to be some clear purpose and end for which his life and ministry had been made, and which was now drawing everything together.

As in relation to his work so there seemed an emerging convergence in his domestic arrangements. In 1961 her own advancing years meant that it seemed an appropriate moment for Sylvia to be nearer her daughter, so the house at Buxted was sold and she moved into a flat in Blackheath. Although Gilbert maintained his room at St Alphege, increasingly his weekend time was spent in Blackheath with Sylvia, where on Sundays they worshipped together at All Saints and in some ways these later years brought them closer together.

From 1962 Gilbert's world was to be centred upon Oxford. As a confessor extraordinary he began to get to know members of the community much more closely than hitherto, helping some of them prepare for profession. In July he gave the first of his major retreats to the community at Burwash. *Consecration* is 124 pages long, a closely-argued work based on the Book of Revelation with a preface devoted to giving instruction to those making a retreat. The work acts as a kind of interface between the traditional western ascetical approach to prayer, which had been a characteristic of his teaching for many years, and an increasing need to understand history as being under judgement. A masterpiece of its kind it may nevertheless have dismayed some of its hearers simply by virtue of its length and the way in which it seeks to deal with a number of different levels of theological concern simultaneously. It was therefore providential that within the community there was one sister who combined an ability to recognize the glory and worth of his teaching with an awareness of the difficulties many of her sisters were having in assimilating it. Sr Marjorie therefore became Gilbert's unofficial secretary and amanuensis, recording his homilies, addresses and retreats, going over them with him and then duplicating them for the community to read and pray at their leisure. It is thanks to her that so much of the material produced by Gilbert has been preserved for use by later generations.

Not all the sisters took to his style. Whilst some responded instinctively, others found little that triggered off a response within them, although amongst this latter group most did find his personal counsel invaluable. It seems certain that most of the community were somewhat in awe of him, though in the course of the following years they came to see an astonishing warmth beneath the somewhat forbidding exterior.

1962 was the year in which *Soundings* was published, a collection of radical essays by Cambridge men and edited by Alec Vidler which served as the vanguard of the 'new theology', the flagship of which was to be Bishop John Robinson's *Honest to God*, which appeared in March 1963. Unlike so many who were to be critical of these works, Gilbert took the trouble of reading and studying them. He was particularly critical of Robinson's use of Bonhoeffer, though he reserved his greatest criticisms for the way in which the writers made use of secular disciplines, especially psychology. His greatest lament over these books was that in what he described as 'our typical Anglican weakness' they seemed to consist of opinions masquerading as theology, an inevitable development in the life of a Church which was becoming more and more isolated from its theological roots. The proper response to them was not to engage in heresy hunting but to continue to work and pray for the renewal of the contemplative life and not just an abstract activity seeking to gain intellectual approval and acceptance from secular disciplines. Well did Evagrius of Pontus say that the true theologian is the one that prays truly. It is perhaps significant in the light of the theological furore surrounding the publication of *The Myth of God Incarnate* in the 1970s that Gilbert saw the doctrine of the Incarnation and its relation to the central doctrine of the Trinity as being of particular importance to the life of the Church in this age. The foundation of Christian faith lies in the fact of God having acted decisively in Christ in history and not in the gradual unfolding of man's religious consciousness.

Throughout 1963 Gilbert spent more and more time at the convent in Oxford and his role in the life of the community clearly led to a considerable degree of tension with SSJE and Fr Hemming who was officially still warden. In the autumn Fr Hemming resigned to take up new work as head of the Canadian Province of his community and the SLG Chapter met, electing Gilbert as his replacement, the first non-religious to hold the office.

His election was to set in motion the final flowering of Gilbert's life and work. Throughout the preceding year he and Mary Clare had discovered a new depth in their work together within the community and Gilbert had become conscious of a profound sense of what he called coinherence, a coming together of his own vocation as priest with that of the community. He expressed this in a letter to Mary Clare written shortly after receiving the invitation to become warden:

> I think you realise that our crisis has made me feel very much more incorporated in the Community itself – and that it is not only in my responsibilities under God for individuals as confessor but our partnership that has brought me into a responsibility for the future – not only in prayer but as a participation in the increase of obedience to their vocation as a witness to the Church. There can be no going back for them now – I cannot be for them an outside advisor. We stand together as witnessing together . . . community and priest.

Gilbert was now seventy-seven. His journey had been long and at times hard but he sensed that even at this late stage he was finally being made ready for the fulfilment of his life. There must be something hopeful for all of us in the fact that a man had to wait until he was seventy-seven before he was able to begin what was to be the most important work of his entire life. Gilbert may have been delighted but more than anything else he was surprised.

7

Living in the Light of the End
1964–67

The Warden SLG

Becoming warden gave Gilbert the opportunity to conclude his work in London and he spent the Christmas period moving out of St Alphege's, preparing to take up residence at the convent where he lived in St Columba, a small self-contained cottage in the grounds. Although he continued to make regular visits to Sylvia at the weekends, there was hardly a single event in the life of the community in the next three and a half years at which Gilbert did not preach or speak, in addition to his continuing work of giving major retreats to the community. The only outside work he maintained now was in connection with Crawley Down.

Coming to live closer to the community Gilbert was enabled to have a deeper understanding of their life and an important moment in his ministry among them came at the time of the Chapter held at Pentecost 1964. Immediately prior to it on Ascension Day he had preached at the profession of three sisters, an occasion he used in order to address the entire community on the need for self-loss. He reminded them that they were not in the convent to 'make a decent job of things' but that at the heart of their vocation lay a conflict with self at the deepest levels of their being. It was the introduction to a theme he was to develop in the following days and which he took up on the eve of the Chapter at a conference for Mother and senior sisters in St Columba.

He set his words in the context of the failure and collapse of the Church about them in an age he characterized as 'these dark days', a phrase much used in *The Face of Love*. The weakness of the Church lay in its lack of prayer and two courses now lay open to those approaching the Christian faith, one of which would have to be chosen. There was either the possibility of making the religious quest one of an individual search for fulfilment making use of such traditions as proved helpful or in taking what he called the 'prophetic' choice, a seeing the world through the eyes of faith from the point of the End, the Parousia. Contemplatives must choose the latter but they had to know that it involved abandoning the search for personal fulfilment, rather it would mean subjecting the 'I' with all its illusions to the reality of judgement. The religious life was not to be thought of as a retirement from the world in the path of self-perfection, another form of inner search in response to the present world crisis, but the process of self-stripping, that battle with oneself which St Anthony had known in the desert.

This served as the introduction to the central thrust of his conference which was to say to the senior sisters how very surprised and disappointed he was at the low level of contemplation within the community. The reason for this lay in what he described as the unwillingness of some sisters to face up to the necessity of self-loss, to take seriously the necessity of entering the dark night of the senses as St John of the Cross described it. He knew of course that this is the cut-off point for most people in the spiritual life. To get beyond it necessitates a surrender of independence, especially of individual judgement, which people in the present age find so difficult. Nevertheless he believed that in a community which described itself as contemplative there ought to be more sisters who had faced up to this than was in fact the case, and *a fortiori*, if the community was really to be of value to the Church then such a commitment was demanded.

To meet this situation Gilbert urged a return to fundamentals in which there should be an emphasis upon three particular aspects of life. First and foremost there was an urgent need for a deepening of the prayer life of the sisters through a renewed emphasis upon the basics of prayer. This would mean simple instruction on the fundamentals of mental and affective prayer and the movement from this into silence. It would also mean a renewed emphasis upon the importance of *lectio divina*, the reading which acted as the undergirding of the life through being rooted in the Scriptures and Fathers.

The second aspect of renewal upon which emphasis would need to be placed was the recognition of the hierarchical principle of obedience. He seemed to feel that a whole generation of sisters had failed to grasp the notion of 'holy order'; consequently their sense of trust was weak, too weak to prevent an attitude of self-seeking in competition with others along the lines of individual imagination and desire.

The third emphasis needed to be placed upon what he called the 'spiritualizing of the natural', a mental divide in too many of the sisters between the natural and the spiritual. The example he gave concerned the times of recreation which instead of being seen as something which was part of the whole was increasingly viewed as an end in itself, something for each sister to use for self-expression. He urged the senior sisters to 'encourage the sisters in the monotony of the right way. Repeat *ad nauseam* what the life is – to let God do what he wants with you, not what you want'.

He took up these things in addressing the community on the following day. He began by contrasting the natural order and its demands for self-expression (this was in 1964, the dawn of the liberated sixties) with the demands of contemplative life.

Religious, he reminded them, at whatever stage they found themselves were called to go beyond the natural with its hidey-holes and securities of various kinds, and accept the need to be re-formed, indeed transformed, in co-operation with the Holy Spirit.

Gilbert was not so much seeking to impose upon them a pattern than attempting to recall them to their own foundations; if they wished to speak of themselves as bound to the work of prayer, then they ought to be so. What was clear to him, and had been so since his days with Fr William, was that there must be a return to the theological roots of the life in the writings of the Fathers, that one great tradition which needed to find renewed expression within the circumstances of life, whatever they might be. Perhaps not everyone understood it in this way, but he was not seeking to turn the sisters into automatons under his control or that of anyone else. On the contrary he believed with St Teresa that the contemplative life exists to present to God a family of adult persons, not those incapable of thinking for themselves.

Among the dominant concerns of his later years in whatever context he taught was an attempt to encourage people away from a type of prayer which had its origins in the 19th century French manuals into that which is more fully trinitarian, concerned with cosmic redemption and rooted in the Parousia of Christ. He believed too that this understanding of prayer had important consequences for liturgical reform and he looked forward to a time when a powerfully prophetic element would be incorporated into worship. That it was possible he knew from his experience of Orthodox worship but it ran quite contrary to the style then the vogue in anglo-catholic circles. This had been much influenced by Martin Thornton's book *Pastoral Theology: A Re-Orientation*, in which he had argued for emphasis to be placed upon the notion of a holy remnant, a company of refugees with a spirituality appropriate to their condition, an approach of which Gilbert was highly critical.

Eschatology and prayer

Gilbert's own understanding of the prophetic-eschatalogical nature of prayer and the spiritual life was to play a prominent part in his ministry of these last years, and can perhaps be said to be his most important contribution to an understanding of the nature of the church and the nature of prayer. Its origins lay in the Hulsean lectures of J.N. Figgis which gave Gilbert an understanding of the prophetic, a vision of the realities of human history in the light of faith. At one level this gave rise to Gilbert's social involvement in the East End, and especially to his years of ministry in Poplar. It also developed into that deeper understanding of the functional relationship between the temporal and the eternal, the eschatology which so confused his fellow members of the Moot. Only at Fairacres however did it find its full and united expression.

The esssence of this prophetic-eschatology lies in the juxtaposition of a profound awareness of the various crises facing mankind – social, political and ideological, as well as those which threaten man's individual destiny, with a theology wholly rooted in the Biblical revelation of God's purposes in creation, redemption and the coming judgement. Drawing upon passages such as Colossians 1.12–20, Ephesians 1.3–10 or Philippians 2.6–11, the essential dynamic of his understanding lies in the prevenient activity of God in and for his creation. The living God is the Trinity who is drawing the whole of creation into the unity, whereby Christ presents it to the Father perfected as the fruits of his own sacrifice offered once for all on the Cross. Gilbert loved to dwell on the consequences of Christ's having taken the whole manhood to himself at his Incarnation, the whole of humanity from the beginning to the end of human history. He took upon himself also the sin of the whole world and by means of his passion and resurrection became for all mankind a boundless source of light and life for the forgiveness of sins and the healing of all the disorders, individual and social, resulting from sin. All the hidden consequences of Satan's 'I will not serve', have now been brought to light, and the Holy Spirit now 'convinces the world of sin, righteousness and judgement'. It is for the believer then to look to the End in repentance and faith from within the testings of his historical circumstances. He cannot know exactly how the future will unfold, but in the light of Christ's victory can be convinced that all things do indeed work together for good to those who love God. The believer thus witnesses to his union with Christ's passion in his patient endurance of the sufferings of the times, and through this witness the Kingdom of God is made effectively present in those circumstances.

Christians individually and the Church corporately, are called by God to be his suffering servant for the sake of this witness during the whole course of this last age of history, for 'he must reign until he has put all his enemies under his feet' (1 Cor.15.25), and then Christ the End, the eschatological Kingdom of God, will have come.

It is precisely because of this present Parousia of Christ in his witnesses that the whole continuing life of mankind with its various political, economic, social, intellectual and religious structures lies under judgement, for they manifest a man-centredness which conflicts with God's activity. The judgement of God, if man will accept it, is not to condemn the world but to renew it. Thus although Gilbert himself had given much of his life to political and social activities to serve those most in need, he had always been aware that such a work served to do no more than repair a torn fabric, and must in the end give way to the need for the total renewal of the whole creation. Such a renewal is now being accomplished and the work of the Church, and especially those within it called to an extreme witness – both the martyrs to blood and those called to the 'white martyrdom' of contemplative prayer is to prepare corporately and individually to be transformed into a new creation, the Kingdom of God.

Intrinsic to this eschatological thinking is the corporate nature of the faith. Over-emphasis upon the salvation of the individual is untrue to the New Testament and to the tradition of the Church. Salvation is corporate as well as personal, it is for the whole creation, and therefore the renewal of the Church has always to be for the renewal of the corporate life of mankind and not just to serve the pious needs of individuals. This emphasis upon the corporate underlies Gilbert's teaching on the nature of the Church. For him the Church could never be reduced to an institution or a convenient form for the organization of religious practice. It was always the Body of Christ in which Christ himself continued to be actively present as head, ruler and protector of his body. It was thus the created image of the Holy Trinity, and central in itself to the Lord's whole work of redemption in drawing the creation into unity. In this respect the Church plays a central part in the eschatological purposes of God. No doubt his grasp of this was heightened by his contacts with Orthodox theology, especially in the person of Vladimir Lossky but it is equally true that for their part, the Orthodox were drawn to him because of his eschatological emphasis.

There can be no doubt that not all who heard him understood it, but one of the hallmarks of the teaching of Gilbert at every stage of his ministry was the attempt to teach prayer within the boundaries of this eschatological framework. It was only in the last couple of years of his life that he was finally able to say exactly what he needed and wanted to say, and had a community, many of whom were able and willing, to hear it.

He did hope that an understanding such as this could be allowed to give shape to the Church's liturgy, but in the early 1960s attempting to reform the liturgy was somewhat more complex than it has subsequently become. He was however setting out some of the necessary theological and ascetic foundations for that reform even though he was unlikely ever to be able to participate in them. Too often liturgical reform has been a 'lowest common denominator' refurbishing rather than an attempt to give renewed expression to a prophetic faith. He stressed that liturgical reform should flow out of the experience of common prayer and placed emphasis upon the relationship between the Eucharist and the divine office rather than seeing them as separate. Without such emphases liturgical reform is bound to end up as nothing more than the work of technicians.

Crawley Down

It is worth noting that at Crawley Down since the late 1970s considerable liturgical reform has been carried out in the light of Gilbert's teachings and with some considerable success, though in the early 1960s the possibility that this might have been happening at Crawley Down appeared somewhat unlikely. There had been a presence there since 1938 and a monastic community since 1953, ostensibly set apart for the work of contemplative prayer with an overspill of service. Little seemed to be happening however and whenever signs of life appeared they almost at once petered out. Fr Robert, whilst never wholly disclaiming the notion of contemplative for CSWG, nevertheless found it somewhat inappropriate to himself. In the later fifties and early sixties he began to withdraw into himself and was often said to be unwell or tired.

It seemed to Gilbert that the basic problem at Crawley Down was a misunderstanding of the nature of contemplative prayer. Too often it has been seen as something initiated by ourselves in response to God rather than as something worked within us by God and for which, at the most, we can prepare by the appropriate ascetic discipline of the Church.

At a time when activism was in the ascendancy it is perhaps not altogether surprising that enclosed religious should wish to have some part in the action. Some, and certainly this can be said of Fr Robert, wished to engage in the overspill of service as guides of the spiritual life without first having themselves submitted to all that the life involves, and had they done so they would probably have been less willing to set themselves up in this way. No doubt Gilbert recalled that before St Seraphim of Sarov became a great director of souls he had spent fifteen years as a hermit, and that the writings of St John of the Cross were the fruit of much suffering. Thus if religious wanted to be more active then it was in the work of prayer in which they should be so. He frequently recalled Fr William's words about the mission of the Church being weak because its prayer was weak. If religious wanted to participate in the building up of the Church in the world then there was an enormous amount of repair work to be accomplished and collapsing structures to be dealt with which would be best served by contemplatives playing their own part in the whole mission by attending yet more assiduously to their own vocation of prayer.

Although appearances were not promising, it seems that Gilbert never abandoned his vision of what CSWG might become. He saw their experience of apparent failure as a sign of their being tested and nothing is more certain a sign of God's intending grace than a time of testing. This period came to a head in 1966 with a major crisis within the community. Some of the trustees wished to bring in an outside Superior but this was resisted by Gilbert. Instead Fr Robert stepped back, and a young monk from New Zealand, Fr Gregory Dudding, was appointed Pro-Superior.

The community in its own official papers since that time has seen itself as the successor to what Fr William was seeking to found within the Church of England and names Gilbert as the community's spiritual theologian and, together with Fr William and Fr Robert as one of its founders. It is clear from letters written to the new Superior early in 1967 that Gilbert accepted this understanding of his own role and that although he realized he would not live to see it, he clearly saw CSWG as the place where Fr William's vision of a contemplative community for men would be fulfilled. To this end along with Fr Robert he gave his agreement to five principles for the community's life and development drawn up in 1967.

It is perhaps worth while briefly considering what has happened to CSWG since the time of Gilbert's death as an example of a community which has in fact consciously sought to shape its life in accordance with his teachings. Certainly a fair test of any writer or teacher is to consider some years after his death whether there has been an abiding quality to his work, or whether it has been of merely passing worth. Reference has already been made to various groups who could look back upon Gilbert Shaw's work and recognize its qualities but what value has it for the present and the future? Does it in any way, to use his own theme, show itself to be part of a living tradition which can continue to feed the Church in a subsequent age?

In the years from 1967 the small community under the leadership of Fr Gregory continued to be guided by Gilbert's teachings. They were regularly read aloud and one of the monks undertook the task of collecting and cataloguing his complete works. At first sight it might have appeared that little in the community was changing; numbers remained static and small; but over a long period significant changes began to be perceptible, most notably in the development of worship and the pattern of the ordering of the daily life, and by the late 1970s there was a clear increase in the numbers of those coming to test their vocation and staying.

In October 1979 the original community member and founder Fr Robert died, and almost as if this marked a major transition stage, some months later the monastery was engulfed by a fire which destroyed all the living area and the library, leaving only the chapel and a small area which housed the kitchen, refectory and two guest rooms. The monks had to live in caravans or on mattresses in rooms hastily partitioned by curtains and one wondered after more than forty years just what it all meant. It seems to have been a turning-point however. The insurance money meant it was possible to build a new (and considerably warmer) community house, to which was added a guest-wing with a library which could also serve as an appropriate place for conferences and quiet days. There has also been a marked increase in the number of men joining the community and the establishment of a group of what are called Seekers, whereby men can come and live at the monastery for a year to have time to consider the questions of their life and vocation. Some of these have joined the novitiate whilst others have been enabled to return to their work enriched and better equipped for service.

By 1984 there was a crisis about too many people and too little space to house them – a complete change from the previous years of faithful living, and something which seemed to call in question the community's ability to remain small enough to maintain a hidden and silent life given above all to the work of prayer. Consideration began to be given to the possibility of opening another community house.

'Monks in the City'

With his firm belief in the hierarchy of obedience in the Church, Gilbert would no doubt have approved of the fact that a way forward was presented by the community's diocesan and Visitor, the Bishop of Chichester, Dr Eric Kemp. He was concerned about the particularly difficult 'inner-city' area of Brighton, including the Brunswick district of Hove, where the Church had all but collapsed. Might it be possible for the community to open a house in the parish close by the parish church of St Patrick to live in the urban desert as a contemplative community undergirding by its prayer and presence the work of a new parish priest and his family? This came at just the time when the Church of England had begun to consider its response to the problems associated with inner-city deprivation, resulting in the publication of the report *Faith in the City*. The community considered this summons from their bishop and as an adventure in faith agreed to send six monks to found a new house, the Monastery of Christ the Saviour which was inaugurated on the feast of Corpus Christi 1985.

The contrast between a monastery in the woods and that in a six-storey terrace could not be greater but in the short time since the venture began there are signs that it is been greatly blessed and that what was once a parish facing redundancy is now a lively centre for the renewal of the area, in which the community of monks plays its own particular part.

Many of the developments in worship which had become a feature of life at Crawley Down have now come to play an important part in the life of St Patrick's and, although requiring some adaptation from the monastic to the parish community, have brought a whole new approach to worship.

The dark interior of the church has been transformed by the removal of the pews and the positioning of a central worship area focused upon the altar and an icon of the Holy Trinity, around which pews have been placed in a large circle. As at Crawley Down the weekly pattern of worship is based upon an unfolding of the Paschal mystery. An evening Mass of the Last Supper on Thursdays is followed by Bible study groups meeting together in the Church recalling the teaching of Jesus to his disciples 'on the night in which he was betrayed'. On the following morning there is a period of silent prayer before the cross from 6.00am, beginning a day of simple fasting and prayer which concludes with an evening service which combines the veneration of the cross and the liturgy of the Pre-sanctified Gifts. Each Saturday the Mass at midday is followed by a shared parish meal, part of the preparation for the Sunday celebration of the Resurrection. Sunday afternoons include a special 'Come and See' event in which those unfamiliar with the parish have the opportunity to share in something of its life.

The additional space within the church provided by the extensive alterations has allowed the development of another important feature of life at St Patrick's. This is the welcome being offered to the many wayfarers and homeless who drift to the south coast. The church is kept open day and night, and bedding is provided for those who choose to sleep there at night, together with food and drink. It means that whilst worship is being offered at the heart of the building, simultaneously love for the brethren, of a most practical kind, is being provided literally alongside.

Already in the short time since the new work has begun it is being recognized as something which can offer hope to others in similar situations and in the coming years there will clearly be many people coming to see just what is happening at St Patrick's, and at a time when the catholic wing of the Church has appeared negative in many of its attitudes, it represents a major positive contribution to the hope of renewal for the Church in urban priority areas.

In a quite unexpected way, this new development of CSWG has brought together the prophetic teaching of Gilbert Shaw and a commitment to city life which was so prominent a part of his own ministry, as well as that of Fr William before him. It is also saying to the Church as a whole that if there is to be an adequate response to the needs of such areas, then it must be based upon a theological and spiritual renewal of the Church. Reorganization alone will not make it possible to survive what it is no exaggeration to call an urban desert. For this reason the accommodation at the monastery is being developed so that ordinands and others concerned with urban ministry will be able to pursue guided theological study within this new context which has brought together urban mission and the contemplative monastic life.

Closely related to this concern for theological renewal as the undergirding of any structural reform, the CSWG community under the guidance of Gilbert's life and teaching has also initiated two further developments. The first is an Associateship which offers not just a link with the community and a measure of spiritual direction built around a personal rule of life, but is seeking to be a way of taking the particular theological formulation of the community into the parishes and the local Eucharistic communities. Gradually, although not in quite the same way, something of the renewal enjoyed in Hove is also being experienced in a number of other places, urban and rural. It is also interesting to note that this is drawing in men and women of quite different traditions and denominations who are discovering in the recovery of theology within the One Great Tradition an enrichment of their own previous experience.

The second development is a course of study in theology in relation to the recovery of the One Great Tradition for Associates and others, including one of the lay monks, for whom it has been accepted as a course of study leading to ordination. In such ways it seems that Gilbert's claim that he was setting up a theological loom for a subsequent generation is beginning to bear fruit through the agency of the CSWG community. As we have seen, Gilbert was scathing about the so-called theological reformation of the early 1960s and of the period subsequent to his death he would certainly have found himself in agreement with the late Fr Alexander Schmemann who wrote:

> . . . I have the strange impression that seldom in the past has our theology been more isolated from the Church.

> Seldom has it had less impact in our life, has it been so exclusively a 'theology for theologians' as today. . . . Why is this so? . . . It is, I am convinced, its failure to reveal the true meaning and therefore the power, the saving and transforming power, of the genuine Orthodox Tradition within the context of our present situation, to make it into a consistent critique of, but also an answer to, the values, the world-view and the way of life which stem from today's spiritual and intellectual crisis. (*Church, World, Mission* SVS Press, pp 16f)

It may well be in some places that the possibility of the 'saving and transforming' power of the one great tradition is now indeed beginning to be experienced in a way directly related to Gilbert's own efforts to teach and direct others in its light.

The solitary vocation

It was at Fairacres however that Gilbert was setting up the loom, the place where he was enabled to give his teaching and where it was able to be received and recorded, and it was together with the community there that he set in motion a new development in the life of the Church which may prove to be his most significant legacy to subsequent generations. This was his concern for those who experience a call to the solitary life.

Although there has always been a recognizable place for those called to live the solitary life in the western Church they have not been accorded the same significance as they have in the East. Within the Church of England since the time of the Oxford Movement there have been individuals here and there who have lived this vocation. Fr William ministered to Sr Adeline Cashmore, one of a tiny number of women who have experienced a call to live as a recluse given to intercession and prayer. The nature of the life is its hiddenness but Gilbert looked to the possibility of the provision of support and canonical recognition for any who showed evidence of such a vocation. As he understood the great tradition, hermits should be seen as an ordinary part of the Church and that wherever the Church was, there would be those given the grace to seek and live the life. Recognizing and meeting this need would be another way of fulfilling the contemplative role in the mission of the entire Church.

It is clear that this concern for the recovery and development of the solitary life figured highly in the sharing between Gilbert and Mary Clare. In a letter to her in mid-1962 he expressed what he regarded as essential to the solitary vocation:

> The point about the Solitary is not that it is the best or a special form of individual excellence but is a particular representation of the coinherence in the One life of the whole – a whole dedication of self to represent and reflect the unity – in which the separation of the natural is most fully brought into the realisation that all man is one in Christ.

He later echoed this in a homily saying of the Solitary that:

> for him solitude is the milieu of his growth in a mature relationship with God and in the knowledge of God's will for the world. For him, withdrawal emphasises the fact of his relationship with men, because through the deepening of his prayer in solitude he comes to a deeper realisation of the coinherence of mankind.

Intercession for the world lies at the heart of the solitary vocation. A favourite saying of Gilbert's which he often quoted, was from the Epistle to Diognetus: 'As the soul is to the body, so are Christians to the world, to give it life and to keep it in life'. He applied this to solitaries in seeing their vocation as serving to sustain the other contemplatives, just as they in their turn sustained the rest of the mission of the Church. Thus the renewal of the solitary vocation was an essential and indispensable part of the renewal of the contemplative life in the Church and thus ultimately the renewal of the whole Church.

In 1963, Gilbert and Mary Clare shared this concern with Archbishop Michael Ramsey who gave his support to the idea that they should take this a stage further together with Fr Sophrony, who had himself once been a hermit on Mt Athos and had also ministered to other hermits. He was brought to Fairacres and they put to him their understanding of the vocation and their hopes for the establishment of a settlement of solitaries, a *lavra*, the first members of which would be sisters who had already been living a life of prayer in stability for some time and who now wished to test their vocation to this new life. Their aim would be to establish a life based firmly upon the writings and experiences of the early Fathers of both east and west and to try and discover how forms of the eremetical life could enrich and sustain the recovery of the solitary vocation within the Anglican communion. After some time in silence and prayer, Fr Sophrony declared 'I believe this to be of the tradition and acceptable to God'. A month later the Community Council accepted this as the Holy Spirit's guidance and agreed unanimously:

> that the community is called to go beyond the question of temporary deserts for a few and try to recover for the Church of England the fullness of the Contemplative life in a settlement of solitaries.

This development was a source of constant joy to Gilbert in the last years of his life, not least because it had the support of the Archbishop of Canterbury. Gilbert believed that there could be no real renewal of the Church without there also being the renewal of the episcopacy, for the hierarchical principle he had stressed to the sisters was equally important for the Church as a whole. He greatly enjoyed the archepiscopal visit to Fairacres in 1966 and when Archbishop Michael quoted his favourite verse from the Epistle to Diognetus he took this as a clear sign of God's blessing upon the project. It was his great joy too that when the new foundation was officially blessed in May 1967, it was Archbishop Michael who presided at the dedication, for the community had, after much searching, bought a farmhouse and an oast-house in a pear orchard near Tonbridge in Kent, within the archdiocese of Canterbury.

Gilbert's intention for the new house was that it should be a *lavra*, a settlement of solitaries rather than a place providing for independent solitaries. It also seemed possible to unite these hopes with those of his friend David Shapland, a priest he had known for some years, formerly chaplain to St Catherine's, Cambridge, who wished to find a way of living a community life together with his wife Julie and their family. In addition to the provision for the solitary life this meant that there would also be a form of coenobium centred upon the presence of a married chaplain. The hope was that this would allow for the possibility that the place might become a centre for prayer and study to which Christians, both ordained and lay, might come and enter more deeply into the one great tradition of the spiritual life. For this reason there would need to be a good library. It was this emphasis upon study that led to the choice of the name Bede House for the new foundation, St Bede having been a great scholar and historian.

In October 1965 the Shaplands moved into Bede House and building work began on the rest of the house so that it was possible for the first two sisters to follow in the following August. On St Bernard's day the new chaplain was commissioned at Fairacres and the two sisters sent forth with him (c.f. the homily which forms the appendix below), and in the following May Gilbert, though by now very frail, was able to join them for the official opening by the Archbishop.

In the years since the establishment of Bede House there have been a number of other places where the eremetical vocation has been established, not least by the Franciscans who now look after Glasshampton and maintain hermitages at Shephards Law in Northumberland and Compton Durville in Somerset. All of these would have been a cause of delight to Gilbert and also to Fr William, whose own original community, The Society of the Divine Compassion, was a forerunner of the present Society of St Francis. Of significance too was an ecumenical conference held at St David's, Wales in the autumn of 1975 exploring various facets of the hermit life in both east and west. In a very real way such a conference would not have been possible were it not for the work of Gilbert Shaw a decade earlier.

The theologian

The volume of writings from his last three years is considerable. Largely in the form of homilies and addresses, some are of significance only to religious, but the majority would be of great value to any seeking to live the life of prayer. A series of homilies from the second half of 1966, *Spiritual Warfare* would surely rank among the greatest writings on the spiritual conflict of the purgative way and our participation in the overcoming of evil. They bring his work in regard to such matters to a proper fulfilment, fully incorporating it within the totality of the eschatological teaching though without any repudiation of what had gone before.

In one who spent so much time in ministering to contemplatives, both religious and in the world, an emphasis upon the spiritual conflict is not surprising. Unlike some writers who borrow ideas from popular psychology, he was adamant that in describing this conflict his language was not to be understood metaphorically, as if no more than a description of the process of attempting to deal with inner psychological turmoil, a spiritual attempt at Jungian individuation by confrontation with the shadow. It is not that he was unaware of the work of psychologists, it was rather that he believed their work was limited by their presuppositions about man which did not take into account his being a creature of God now re-created in Christ.

He believed that if we want medical knowledge we should go to a doctor; if we wish to know something about the text of the New Testament we should go to a scholar; if we wish to know about the background to a particular theological dispute we should go to a theologian suitably able to help us; and if we wish to discover something about the realities of the evil one, it is to those living a life of prayer that we should go. The spiritual conflict is the battle for which the Church has been mustered and he felt that it was vital for those called to the contemplative life in particular that they should have a proper understanding of such things if they were to meet the demands of their vocation.

To some, language about angels, demons or the person of the devil acts as an immediate cut-off point. He well understood that this was the case, but his own direct experience of such realities prevented him taking refuge in talk about symbolism or some alternative explanation. Attempts to reduce the experience of the Desert Fathers and saints into 'interesting psychological types' exasperated him. In a letter to Mother Mary Clare in 1962 he commented:

> Here is the difficulty – how much can one say to the average Church of England bishop to carry conviction?

It is certain that his 'Spiritual Warfare' homilies could be of great value to bishops and others in relation to the continuing questions raised by such matters simply because they set them within the context of a properly developed theology of the spiritual life of the Church. It is this approach within which for example, it is properly recognized that the realm of the demonic is under the rule of the Kingdom of God, and must serve it for the testing of the sons of the Kingdom and thus must finally perceive their own futility, that prevents Gilbert's teaching from falling into the excesses and errors of some of the writing to emerge from the charismatic movement. A more difficult question would have to consider whether there were yet any Church of England bishops ready to receive it.

In spite of drawing near to his eightieth birthday he continued diligently in his work as warden, helping sisters to prepare for profession, and for them he produced a work *Religious Profession* suitable not only for those on the verge of taking vows, but for all who wished to renew their dedication and which, according to the present Mother-General of the community 'remains a basic exposition of the Community's understanding of the purpose and practice of its life'. In 1967, by which time he was very frail, he still managed a major series of homilies on the basics of prayer in relation to the vision of the letters to the seven Churches of Asia from the Book of Revelation called *The Increase of Prayer* in addition to the regular homilies and conferences he gave to the community, which as before continued to make great demands of those who heard them.

There are four recurring words or phrases which characterize this last period of teaching. The first is a pair of words: penitence–dependence. These he saw as giving appropriate expression to the particular nature of man before God into which faith leads. Penitence characterizes the response of fallen man in the presence of God, it is the *sine qua non* of all creaturely prayer and leads into the necessity of dependence upon God for the growth of the relationship in prayer. Only such an approach makes Christian prayer Christian.

Closely related to the first is the second word: participation. His powerful awareness of the creative activity of God at work in the Church and the world brought home to him the realization that at the most we are called to work together with God in his work, whether this be in the active work of political struggles for a better social order, or in the life of prayer. In all things we are enabled to do no more than participate in the work which God is already doing: that of drawing all things to their fulfilment and unity in Christ. Once again this marks out Christian prayer as something different from the various Gnostic cults that proliferate, offering to teach methods and schemes of prayer, and stresses the necessity of a close link between doctrine and prayer. After all there is little point in speaking about prayer as a participation unless we are clear what our faith understands by the work of God into which we are being drawn. This was certainly the case with regard to the whole matter of the spiritual conflict and the demonic. Instead of relying upon one's own powers which would inevitably be thereby placed under great strain and almost certainly fail, he increasingly saw that what mattered was a proper setting of the work within the context of the total sharing of the Church in the Lord's overcoming of evil.

The third word is: perseverance. Although he was ever constant in reminding the sisters that contemplative prayer was a gift, for which at the most we can prepare ourselves, and not something that could be achieved or earned, nevertheless it was something that required perseverance. As he discovered at Fairacres, it did not take too much of an effort to go so far along the path of prayer and then to stop, perhaps satisfied with one's achievements. Yet the whole tradition of prayer in the Church, especially as it has been known in the teachings of St John of the Cross, focuses upon the necessity of recognizing that we have never arrived at the final stage, and that instead we are ever called onward. Gilbert often referred the sisters to the words of both St Teresa of Avila and St Seraphim of Sarov to the effect that so few advance in the life of prayer because so few persevere.

A number of Gilbert's former students from Burgh have recalled how emphatic was his teaching on discipline, and that in retrospect this served them well, especially those serving in isolated foreign missionary stations. This finally became an emphasis upon perseverance, for whilst this includes the necessity of discipline, it also goes beyond it. A cold discipline which ends up as a mere formality is not perseverance, though equally there could be no real perseverance which was not founded upon the necessity of discipline. That remains true for the beginner as much as for the mature solitary.

The final word has its origins in the Patristic writings to which he was introduced by Fr William: deification. His growing emphasis upon this was as the result of his overwhelming awareness of the present activity of God towards the unity of creation. Because man is made for unity with God, and indeed not just man but all creation, and all that is now being drawn into that unity through the redemptive activity of Christ, it follows that all spiritual and material life must be directed accordingly. Social commitment is as much a consequence of such an understanding as is the work of the liturgy, and at various times in his life Gilbert was completely caught up in both. Deification is not to be understood as something belonging to the realm of the individual in his or her piety, it is wholly corporate. The work of prayer is not just a manifestation of individual piety but a concern with the unity of all mankind, something of great importance in thinking about the vocation of the solitary. The liturgical work of the Church, in Eucharist and Office is thus to be seen not just as 'services', but as key moments in the Church's participation in the in-breaking of the fulness of the Kingdom. Each Eucharist is an anamnesis not just of Creation, Calvary and Pentecost, but a proleptic experience of the End, and the work of prayer is to be drawn into a fuller participation in that eucharistic living which is the hallmark of all that is called Christian.

The coming end

As early as 1965 his age began to place some limits upon his work and he felt less able to conduct major retreats for the community and had begun to invite one or two priests to help in this, among whom was Fr Percy Coleman who reports the shock he had on discovering that throughout his addresses he would have Gilbert sitting next to him. In fact Fr Percy was one of the priests whom he was slowly drawing into the orbit of the community with a view to ensuring continuity after his death. Another was Fr Donald Allchin. These two were to play a vital part in guiding the community throughout the subsequent twenty years.

Donald Allchin, who served as Gilbert's confessor in his last years, had known him first at conferences of the Fellowship of St Alban and St Sergius during the 1950s and freely admits that he didn't take to Gilbert at first. As with many, the manner prevented him from seeing the real man. By the time he came to know him at Fairacres two things had changed. First of all the experience of rejection and failure of the fifties had served to soften Gilbert's manner somewhat. It is noticeable that photographs of him in the last period of his life tend to show him smiling whereas those of a previous period tended to portray him as stern and forbidding. Second, his time at Fairacres really was the fulfilment of his life and work. At last he had found the community and place in which he could complete that which had been laid upon him. Thus the period of his 'Nunc Dimittis' was a period of relaxation and joy, making him that much easier to come to know and love. Of course Donald still felt somewhat in awe of the man, not least in that sense of total inadequacy that young priests experience when an older and wiser member of the Church comes to make their confession, but he was now able to appreciate and love him whereas previously fear had predominated.

As 1967 wore on it became abundantly clear that he would not have much longer to live although almost right to the end he maintained his personal ministry to the sisters and continued to preach the Sunday homily. As his confessor, Fr Donald has reported how peaceful Gilbert was as he knowingly came towards the time of his death. To Donald's delight on one occasion he said to him: 'You know Donald, we've spoken so much about theology, but in the end what matters above all is love'. In July he baptized his great-grandchild, one of his last acts as a priest for soon after he began his final illness.

Of his dying and death there were three moments of great significance. The first occurred when he was apparently deeply unconscious. Suddenly he 'came to', sat up and gave those gathered around him what has come to be known as the 'last homily'. It contained a number of themes, some of which had been his major concerns for the community: the work of the Holy Spirit as guide of the community; their work of listening and intercession; the need to meet people where they are in order to build up unity. For one whose life had been so committed to words it is perhaps appropriate that even at the end he was not to be denied the last word, and though only two hundred words long it served as a fitting conclusion to his ministry, not just at Fairacres but throughout the preceding forty-three years.

The second moment of note was during a period when Mary Clare was sitting alone with Gilbert. She noticed that although unconscious he was showing clear signs of being engaged in some final psychic conflict; it did not last long but was evidently fierce. The form of the conflict, whether demonic or a final assault from those whom he had done so much to disarm, we cannot know, but it is not altogether surprising that to one who had for so long resisted evil at this level there should come one last attack. That he overcame this assault is clearly indicated in that once it was over he appeared to go into a yet deeper and more peaceful state of unconsciousness and began the final process of dying.

He died on 18 August having first been anointed by Fr Derek Allen and Fr Hugh Wybrew and the third moment of note came shortly after death had occurred. Those present commented on the peculiar nature of his skin. It was not merely that relaxation of the muscles which often accompanies death, bringing with it apparent youthfulness, but an unmistakeable and peculiar transformation of his body, and such a distinct change as to cause one sister to say that 'it was the nearest thing to a death bed transfiguration I've ever seen'. The fact of this unusual occurrence has been testified to by a good number of reliable and trustworthy witnesses both within the community and without. No one has ever known quite what to make of this occurrence but after twenty years the remembrance of the sight continues to be a source of joy to all those who witnessed it. The author recalls from his own experience as a hospice chaplain a similar occurrence in which shortly after death the corpse of a Roman Catholic priest gave the impression of manifesting light. An incarnational theology should not lightly dismiss the possibility that a body which in life had been indwelt by the Holy Spirit may after death continue to manifest the radiance of the Spirit's presence. No doubt we do not see as many people die nowadays as once was common but the words of Wesley ought not be overlooked in considering this account of his death:

> O lovely appearance of death
> What sight upon earth is so fair?
> Not all the gay pageants that breathe
> Can with a dead body compare.

His death was followed by a solemn Mass of Requiem at the convent at which Fr Percy Coleman preached. There had been an enormous number of tributes received at the convent from many different branches of the Christian family. After the service his body was interned in that part of the Oxford cemetery reserved for SLG; thus he was united with the community in death as he had been in life.

Gilbert's legacy to the Church is primarily his teaching, but immediately his will made funds available to the community with which to begin a small printing house, which subsequently has become the SLG Press. It has now produced well over 100 books and booklets on prayer and various aspects of the spiritual life, among them some of Gilbert's own, and is a visible presence within the Church of Gilbert's influence within the community and of his partnership with Mother Mary Clare.

Although at many times he had struggled to make sense of what was happening to and within him, although he had known long years of night and darkness, he never seems to have lost sight of the 'end', that for which he was made. 'Living in the light of the End' could in some measure be held as a suitable title for the central thrust of all Gilbert's teaching. His was a summons to begin and persist in that total work of bearing the judgement of that light on our present that we might more and more be enabled to receive and know that love in the unity of the Trinity. If there is power in his teaching of such things, it is because first he lived it and in the end came to know it in death.

Appendix

(The following is the homily preached at Mass in the convent at Fairacres on 20 August 1966 – the feast of St Bernard. At this Mass the new chaplain of Bede House was commissioned for the work and afterwards the two sisters who were to begin the solitary life there left with him. The homily expresses a great deal of Gilbert's understanding of their vocation and the significance of the contemplative life as a whole.)

Humility is the Way

There shall be a way and even fools shall not err therein (Is.35.8)

This is one of the most comforting texts in the Old Testament, a text of prophetic encouragement which stirs us up to look at the reality of our purpose and to get on and fulfil it. The way is the way of humility in which we know we are nothing and God is all. It is the way of the Commandments and of Love wherein we follow the Lamb as he appoints the way for each of us. It is the way by which God prepares us for himself through the wilderness of the ever-changing world, the world of which we are part. We are not to run away from the world but to keep on the way for the world, to gather every bit of it to God that it may receive his mercy and his judgement.

The way of humility is a straight way, and a way which leads straight to God. It is a way by which, in the particular time we are living and in the particular circumstances in which the providence of God may have placed us, we look to the end. Through losing the self we are led by God to fulfil the self in the righteousness of obedience to his will. We are all bound together in the wholeness of the *laos*, of the people of God. Each one of us follows our particular vocation in the give and take with other vocations as God calls all to serve in the full pattern of his people. The road of humility means not criticizing but loving all those others who are in the way, helping the stumbling, pressing on, looking forward, glorifying God.

As we commemorate St Bernard today we are reminded in the Gospel for an Abbot (Matt.19.27–9) that the sacrifice, whatever it may be in the journey of life, made in humility that God's will be done, is a fulfilling of our Lord's own way. 'I am come to do the Father's will' – utter obedience – 'I am content to do it'. Even in this life there is the hundredfold reward and those who have struggled on the way know the tremendous truth of that promise. They, as the Book of Ecclesiasticus tells us (45.5), are led into the dark cloud of the knowledge of God and to an understanding of the whole purpose of man – that man's purpose is to be the mediator of creation. The purpose of man is to do God's will and that purpose is restored in the new creation. It is an apostolate of service.

The old Sarum collect of an Abbot reminds us that it is for each of us as we live in humility of surrender to God's purpose, to follow the way, 'not to look back or to go astray', but to press on, looking to the end – to union with God and to the unity of all creation.

The way is, first of all, the way of righteousness, fulfilling the commandment to love God with all our heart and with all our strength, and in that total commitment to God to find the love of our neighbour. Inasmuch as we are giving all to God, so we must encourage, lead, draw and serve our neighbour, that he be in the same condition as we are – seeking first the kingdom of God. The love of neighbour is not merely some beneficent act of natural alleviation resulting in self-satisfaction because we have given twopence to a beggar or subscribed to the emotional appeal of some suffering. The world is full of suffering which only God can heal. The love of neighbour is to draw him that he should be as we are, that all should be in complete obedience to God. Surely that is what St Paul means by filling up what is left over of the sufferings of Christ, to continue in time his suffering love to bring in the victory of his kingdom, by, with and in which all is being drawn to unity.

In Christ we are indeed called to fulfil the Law but also to fulfil the New Commandment – to love as he loves us, to love with his love in us as he draws us to an intimacy with himself and so with the Father and the Holy Spirit. He draws us not merely into the dark cloud but into the tremendous stillness of the height of Calvary, and through Calvary to the glory of the New Day.

Here is the importance of Sunday, the perpetual recurrence of the Eastern Morn, the Eighth Day, the New Day. The old is past, the veil of the Temple is rent in twain, the Resurrection is here. That is the good news – the good news of the resurrection from the dead that this present time so greatly needs. The Early Church grasped this fact and the Saturday Night Vigil prepared for the glory of the New Day. The New Day is the beginning of the new week, the life of the new Jerusalem, the heavenly city as it descends to draw the passing into its eternity of love-fulness.

To come back to this earth – we are on the way. From the height of Calvary we go through to the Resurrection as members of the new Body. We see the glory of the kingdom that is coming down into this earth, the kingdom of which we are citizens. No longer are we strangers and pilgrims – dodging about here and there – but fellow citizens with the saints. Traversing the way which leads to eternal life, we are at the same time bringing eternal life here and now into time. This surely is one of the primary witnesses of the Religious Life. The Religious is called to withdrawal that the Holy Spirit of God may flow through the openness of his penitence and the stability of his dependence to bring healing to the fever of the contending interests and excitements of man's natural attempts to express themselves and dominate their environment and that of their neighbours.

I would strengthen my words by quoting from others; first from Donald Allchin. In an article on 'The Holy Spirit in Christian Life' (in *Sobornost* V.3), he discusses the problem of Church unity, and comments on an extract from St Peter Damian thus:

> It is not by accident that this teaching about unity of the Church should come in a treatise which speaks of the solitary life, a form of life whose significance, whose every existence indeed, has for a long time been almost forgotten in the West and not only among Protestants. The life of the hermit, the solitary, i.e. of the monk in the original sense of the word, the one who is alone, has been for centuries almost unknown in our Western Christendom.

We have been so taken up with activity either in doing good works or in defending the Church, that we have tended to forget the one thing necessary – a total dependence on Christ.

Later on Allchin quotes Fr Congreve SSJE, as writing:

> Perhaps none have realized as intensely the saving mystery of fellowship, the love of the brethren, as those whom God has called to live by prayer in the greatest solitude, even in the continual contemplation of the hermit.

On this Fr Allchin comments:

> In such a life we see the primacy of the person over the Church as an institution, and the unity of human nature in Christ in the Spirit. It is no accident that both in the Roman Catholic Church and in our own at the present time, this form of life should be being re-discovered.

The solitary is never alone; he is with God and with all men. St Antony of the desert said 'My life is with men'. The solitary is, perhaps, the most complete answer to the secularism of this age, the idolatry of man's progressive attempt of the creation of himself as the purpose and end of life force. We set humility, the royal road of obedience to the Father's will, against the pride of man.

This morning we thank God that through his providential care we have been led to the beginning of the recovery, not of the solitary life for there have been and indeed are solitaries today in the Church of England, but to the recovery of a settlement of solitaries – a *lavra*, to use the ancient word – in the ordered life of the Church. This lavra will, please God, be blessed next year by the Archbishop of Canterbury as part of the total work of Bede House for which we also pray.

To quote again from Fr Allchin who sums up what I have been trying to teach for many years:

> The life of the hermit reproduces in our own time the supreme paradox that it is in the moment of utmost isolation and complete apparent uselessness, in the desolation of the Cross, that the Lord is able to bring about the atonement and reconciliation of man with God. We see here that the Cross is

> lifegiving, and we see here something of the meaning of the 'mounting of the Cross' which is at the heart of the monastic life.

'Apparent uselessness' – the murmurers will say that it is utter nonsense that some women are being tucked away in a corner of a pear orchard, and that a priest who ought in their opinion to be rushing hither and thither in active works in parochial duties, is expecting people to come to Bede House to talk about spirituality. No doubt they would have said the same of those who stood by the Cross: Mary, mother of the Lord, Mary the great penitent, and John the faithful priest.

Those who have known the way of prayer, being led into the dark cloud, know the truth of 'the supreme paradox that it is at the moment of utter isolation and complete apparent uselessness in the desolation of the Cross that the Lord is able to bring about the atonement and reconciliation of man with God' to restore man to his purpose of mediatorship. To this purpose you all, as Sisters of the Love of God, are committed; your attention is focused on repairing; your life is dedicated to that end and you must learn how to stand at the Cross. It is a long learning, it is a long road, but it is a sure road if it is up the hill to Calvary, a road with the dawning knowledge of the glory that descends, which you by being stripped of all self may mediate to the dying world.

Let me repeat again the last sentence of the quotation from Fr Allchin:

> We see here that the Cross is lifegiving, we see something of the 'mounting of the Cross' which is at the heart of the monastic life.

Our place is in that terrible stillness where by, with and in the showing forth of the Lord's death, all men are drawn into the eternal unity. We therefore pray that in the tribulations of this age, the Church as the true reflection of its Head in sacrifice and service may be restored to unity.

One word to our sisters who take us with them into the solitary place. We do not send them out of the Community; they are our ambassadors in the place of solitude to which God is calling them.

To them I would say, take a simple word of St John of the Cross with you as you go. You are dedicated to love and to repairing – that you have been learning with us. Now perhaps you will put it into greater practice than was possible for you in the coenobitic life. 'To love', writes St John of the Cross, 'is to labour – to detach and strip yourself for God's sake of all that is not God'. You in your solitude are not alone; how can you be alone, for you are always with God; you are always under the observation of all those who are with God, for no longer are you or we strangers and pilgrims, but fellow citizens with the saints of God.

You are never absent from the wide world around and its confusion, and above all, you cannot get away from yourself. It is in solitude that the battle with self is fully joined, there is no escape. It is in solitude and silence that we come to know the terror of judgement and are brought to realize that God's mercy is always claiming the wholeness of man's assent to the Love that created and would re-create man's being.

My daughters, your free will is taking you to the solitary life where the greatest battle of all will be with your self. Remember the parable of St John of the Cross in *The Dark Night*. The log is brought in from the forest, damp and moss-grown, its bark full of creeping things. It is put on the fire and, being damp, smells and gives off fumes until it is dried out. So with us – our whole life seems to dry out in the darkness of the senses and then, later, in the far deeper darkness of the spirit for the spirit must be purified that there be nothing of me but all of God.

First you must endure the dryness; the whole sap of self, the love of self, the expression of self, must be dried out of the life before it can burn with the flame of love. There is a delightful story in the *Paradise of the Fathers*. On an occasion when a number of the old men, and some of the younger too, were gathered together in the Church on the Sunday, someone asked them what was the greatest temptation. The old men answered, 'The temptation to get out of the life' – the spirit of seduction being allowed to test the obedience of the still waiting on God as if God seemed to be asking too much. We all know that temptation. The answer is the way of humility; the affirmation that I have given all to God and therefore there would be no point in straying out of the way into the wilderness of the general fog all around. Therefore press forward. There will also be temptations to wonder if you are meant to be there, but you must stand and go on standing that you may be dried out.

As you begin to be dried out, the fire will begin to get hold of you and there will be fitful flames, glimpses here and there of wonderful knowledge as the murky clouds of the self lift in patches. You will know something of the Holy Spirit of God and feel his breath. The oxygen of the spiritual air will fan your log and there will be a flame here and a flame there. What is the end? The end is that the whole of your rotten tree that you give to God becomes one living flame of fire. 'Thus it is dry and it dries; it is hot and heats; it is bright and gives brightness' (*Dark Night*, Book II.Ch.10.1).

Please God that end may be reached this side of judgment, this side of death. Death is a wonderful thing, it is God's harvesting of what you offer him in this life. The consummation at the end of the world will be God's harvesting of all.

We pray for you as you go forth that you may become a still flame for God. We pray for Bede House that it may become a place of light and refreshment, a living centre for the spread of spiritual knowledge. We pray for ourselves that we may be more completely given to God to whom be the glory and the power and the dominion, now and for ever, world without end.

Index